D1015766

DRUGS the facts about

THE A-Z
OF DRUGS

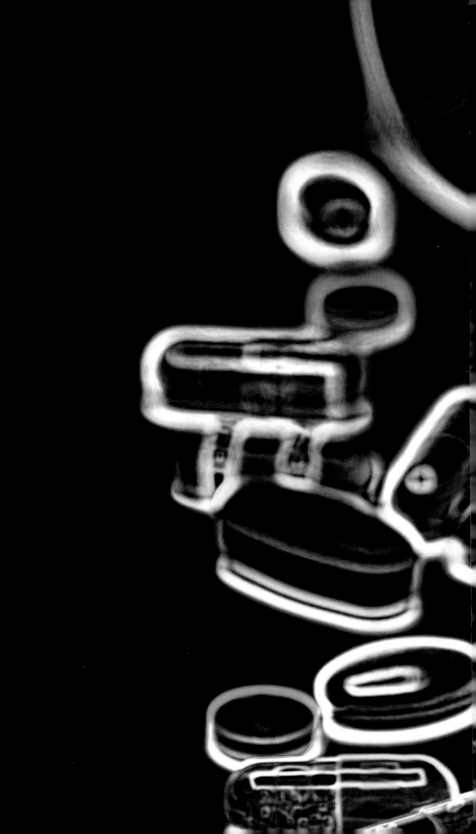

DRUGS the facts about

THE A-Z OF DRUGS

CORINNE NADEN

Marshall Cavendish
Benchmark
New York

Acknowledgment:
Thanks to John Roll, Ph.D., Director, Washington Institute for Mental Illness Research and
Training, Washington State University, for his expert review of this manuscript.

Marshall Cavendish Benchmark
99 White Plains Road
Tarrytown, NY 10591
www.marshallcavendish.us

Library of Congress Cataloging-in-Publication Data

Naden, Corinne J.
The A-Z of Drugs/ by Corinne J. Naden.
p. cm. — (Drugs)
Includes bibliographical references and index.
ISBN-13: 978-0-7614-2673-8
1. Drugs—Juvenile literature. 2. Drugs of abuse—Juvenile literature.
I. Title. II. Series.
RM301.17.N33 2006
615'.1—dc22

2007002267

Photo Research by Joan Meisel
Cover photo: Robert Mullan/Alamy
Alamy: 1, 2-3, 5 Robert Mullan; 6, Judith Collins; 11, Dale O'Dell;
16, Steve Allen; 20, Kim Karpeles; 32, allOver photography; 36, f1
online; 56, J. Richards; 58, Elmtree Images; 65, 90, David Hoffman
Photo Library; 80, Garry Gay; 102, imagebroker; Corbis: 28, Barbara
Walton/epa; 46, Hekimian Julien/Corbis Sygma; 106, Floris Leeumenberg/
The Cover Story; 119, Scott Frei.

Publisher: Michelle Bisson
Art Director: Anahid Hamparian
Series Designer: Sonia Chaghatzbanian

Printed in Malaysia
1 3 5 6 4 2

CONTENTS

ASPIRIN WAS FIRST PUT INTO PILL FORM IN 1900. HOWEVER, HUMANS BEGAN TAKING DRUGS IN THE FORM OF POWDERS, LIQUIDS, AND SMOKE LONG BEFORE THAT.

INTRODUCTION

Humans began using drugs thousands of years before the development of healing drugs such as aspirin and harmful illegal ones such as heroin and LSD. In many ancient cultures, people made use of plants to soothe their pains and cure their illnesses. Since the first human decided to smoke the dried leaves of the hemp plant, people probably used some now-outlawed drugs in controlled ways during ancient rituals as well. Archaeologists have even discovered a clay tablet from Sumer, called a *pharmacopeia,* that dates back to about 2000 BCE. It is the oldest existing catalog of ancient medications.

Plant-based drugs have a long history, and many are used to this day. During the nineteenth and twentieth centuries, the discovery that opium,

7

made from poppies, could produce feelings of euphoria, led to its acceptance in societies as different as China and the United States. However, unmanageable social problems due to drug use also led to the control of opium. China fought two wars in the mid–1800s to prevent England from flooding China with opium. The United States also discovered that opium use could tear apart families and create unproductive workers.

By the early twentieth century, the United States banned opium for recreational use. Yet the potential for huge profits has not stopped people from cultivating poppies for illicit use. Today, farmers make much more money from growing opium poppies than from growing food crops in such countries as Colombia and Afghanistan. Huge profits from the illegal drug trade sometimes fund terrorism and illegal weapons' trade around the world. And the decades' old problem of drug dependency on opium-derived drugs, heroin in particular, continues in many countries, including the United States.

Modern pharmacology of both legal and illegal drugs truly developed over the last two centuries. Today, most drugs are the products of chemical synthesis, although drugs from plants or minerals are still important. Familiar modern drugs fall into three broad categories: prescription, over the counter, and illegal. Prescription drugs are those that doctors prescribe and pharmacists dispense to treat various medical conditions. Over-the-counter drugs are a second category. Customers may purchase such drugs—cough medicine and some pain relievers, for example—without prescription in pharmacies and other stores. Illegal drugs that users purchase from drug dealers, and the misuse and trade of prescription drugs, occupy a third category. Their side effects and/or overdose effects make them extremely dangerous and unpredictable.

Drugs in every category are easy to find. Whether doctor-prescribed or sold over the counter, legal, health-enhancing drugs fill the shelves of pharmacies, medicine cabinets, and grocery stores. Unfortunately, illegal, health-compromising drugs are nearly everywhere, too. Too many of them are found in the hands of drug dealers and drug users in small-town neighborhoods, cities, rural areas, and near or in some schools.

Whether in pill form, liquid, or smoke, whether swallowed, injected, or inhaled, certain drugs contain psychoactive chemical substances. That is, they not only affect an individual's physical state but his or her feelings and moods. In health-enhancing ways, psychoactive drugs can make pain bearable or lift someone's depression. Other drugs—stimulants and antidepressants, for example—help those suffering from anxiety, depression, or mood disorders to cope with their emotional highs and lows. Anesthetics and narcotics ease pain, while calming sedatives can temporarily help people get the sleep they need.

However, some of these very drugs, and drugs that mimic them, impact lives negatively as well. When users take overdose quantities of legal drugs, combine them with an incompatible drug, or consume illegal drugs, the results can lead to dependence or even death. Misused legal drugs and illegal drug use have ruined lives. Each year, illicit drug use costs society billions of dollars in drug-related crime, in lost productivity of drug-using students and employees, in medical care for drug-dependent users, and in government efforts to stop drug traffic and drug abuse.

Government agencies in the United States work to regulate the availability of drugs. These regulations cover legal drugs, such as the nicotine in cigarettes, and illegal ones, such as marijuana and cocaine. One form of regulation is the Controlled Substances Act of 1970, which classifies many drugs according to their dangerous effects and potential for abuse.

The Drug Enforcement Administration (DEA) may start an investigation of a drug any time that it receives data from state and local law agencies or law enforcement laboratories. The information is sent to the Assistant Secretary of Health of the Health and Human Services Department. After evaluation, the DEA receives notification of whether the drug should be controlled and into what classification it should be placed.

Not included under the act are beer, wine and spirits, and tobacco. Many people regard this as a huge loophole since alcohol and tobacco are the country's two most widely used and abused drugs.

Parents, educators, politicians, researchers, doctors, and law enforcement agencies concerned about public health also take action in controlling drugs with abuse potential. Public health agencies publicize warnings about the overuse of legal drugs and the abuse of illegal ones. Health educators

WARNING LABELS ON MEDICATIONS, ANTI-DRUG ADS ON TELEVISION, HEALTH EDUCATION IN SCHOOLS, AND GOVERNMENT REGULATIONS ARE ALL PART OF AN EFFORT TO WARN THE PUBLIC ABOUT THE RISKS OF TAKING DRUGS.

Controlled Substances Act (CSA)

In 1970, as Title II of the Comprehensive Drug Abuse Prevention and Controlled Act, Congress passed the Controlled Substances Act (CSA). Under it, the United States government regulates the manufacture, importation, possession, and distribution of certain drugs.

The CSA creates five different classifications, called Schedules, into which drugs are placed. Some states have added Schedule VI. Substances included are not drugs in the conventional sense but are known to be abused, such as spray paints and inhalants with nitrous oxide (found in aerosol cans and some medical aerosols). The classifications are decided on the basis of a drug's accepted medical use, its potential for abuse, and its potential for creating dependence in a user.

Drug criteria:

Schedule I. High potential for abuse

- No current medical use in the United States
- Lack of accepted safety for the drug use under medical supervision
- Some drugs in this classification: Ecstasy, GHB, heroin, methaqualone

Schedule II. High potential for abuse

- No current medical use in the United States; or accepted medical use with severe restrictions
- Abuse may lead to severe psychological/physical dependence

- Some drugs in this classification: amphetamines (moved from Schedule III to II in 1971), cocaine, Ritalin

Schedule III. Abuse potential less than Schedules I or II

- Currently accepted medical use in the United States
- Abuse may lead to moderate/low physical or high psychological dependence
- Some drugs in this classification: Anabolic steroids, Ketamine, Xyrem (used to treat narcolepsy), Marinol (for nausea in AIDS patients)

Schedule IV. Low potential for abuse as compared with Schedule III drugs

- Currently accepted medical use in the United States
- Abuse leads to limited physical/psychological dependence
- Some drugs in this classification: Valium, long-acting barbiturates

Schedule V. Low potential for abuse as compared with Schedule IV drugs

- Currently accepted medical use in the United States
- Abuse leads to limited physical/psychological dependence as compared with Schedule IV
- Some drugs in this classification: cough medicines with codeine, diarrhea-treating drugs with small amounts of opium

share the latest research about drugs so that students are well informed about the dangers of the most common drugs—alcohol, marijuana, and misused prescription drugs.

The media, too, play a part in educating the public about the benefits and dangers of various drugs. Lawsuits have compelled tobacco companies to stop misleading the public about the health risks of smoking and pay million-dollar settlements to states. States, in turn, have created ad campaigns publicizing the dangers of cigarette smoking. Tobacco companies, as well as distillers of hard liquor, can no longer advertise their products on network television. Black box warnings on the dangers of smoking and drinking appear on billboards, cigarette packs, pill bottles, and in public service ads. Many organizations—Mothers Against Drunk Driving (MADD) and Students Against Destructive Decisions (SADD), for example—speak out loudly, publicly, and regularly about the many ways drugs such as alcohol and marijuana can harm young people.

In the last few years, sports writers have exposed steroid use by some professional athletes to increase their performance and muscle strength. Reporters have written about how steroid use has become rampant among some college and high school players as well. The medical community, too, has been warning about the dangers of steroids, which can cause growth problems, serious heart and liver damage, as well as dramatic negative personality changes in a steroid user.

The messages are everywhere. Learning the way illegal drugs work and how they affect the mind and body help us to understand the place and role of drugs in everyday life. Legal drugs used for the purposes for which they were developed can improve someone's quality of life. Legal and illegal drugs used in unintended ways can harm a person in unintended ways as well.

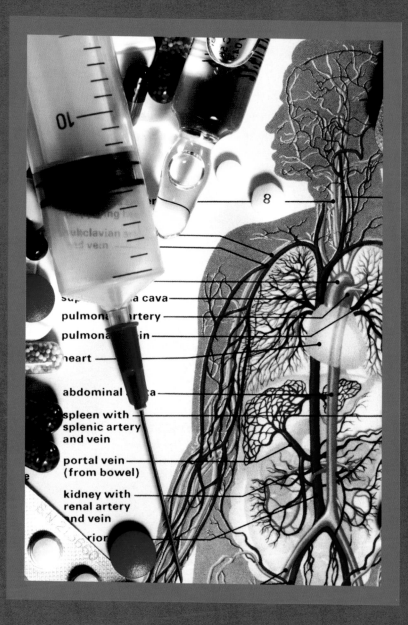

ALL PSYCHOACTIVE DRUGS AFFECT MANY SYSTEMS IN THE BODY. ONCE A DRUG PASSES THROUGH THE BLOOD-BRAIN BARRIER, THE DRUG MAY SPEED UP OR SLOW DOWN BRAIN ACTIVITIES AND LEVELS OF IMPORTANT BRAIN CHEMICALS.

1 DRUG CLASSIFICATIONS

The National Institute on Chemical Dependency, (NICD) classifies controlled substances that have the potential for dependence and abuse. Each drug in a class shares similar ingredients and produces similar effects on the body. These groups include: alcohol, anabolic steroids, cannabis (marijuana), depressants, hallucinogens, inhalants, narcotics, and stimulants. NICD does not list a classification for nicotine. However, many other health groups do. Occupying their own classifications, alcohol, anabolic steroids, and nicotine are listed alphabetically with other drugs, beginning in Chapter 2.

Cannabis

The *cannabis* classification includes marijuana, its active ingredient THC, and hashish. Marijuana tops the list of the most commonly abused illegal drugs in the United States. It is a mixture of the dried leaves, seeds, flowers, and stems of the hemp plant *cannabis sativa.*

Marijuana has been used for centuries. The ancient Hindus, Persians, and Assyrians knew it, and used it in some religious ceremonies. In fact, it has a long history of use in rituals around the world. Some doctors prescribed the drug—then called cannabis—in the nineteenth century to relieve various kinds of pain or to induce sleep. Supposedly, England's Queen Victoria took it on the advice of her physician to treat certain pains. But when the drug's potentially addictive qualities began to be recognized, a United States federal ban stopped most legal marijuana use in 1937.

Until 2005 when the Supreme Court banned the use of medical marijuana, certain patients in some states could use the natural drug medicinally. Marijuana has shown some benefit for people with the eye disorder glaucoma, which is characterized by too much pressure in the blood vessels of the eye. Substances in marijuana may lower this pressure, though further studies are needed. Marijuana's active ingredient, THC, has had other medicinal uses. It can stimulate appetite and relieve nausea. Underweight HIV/AIDS patients and cancer patients enduring chemotherapy have used natural marijuana to improve their appetites in order to gain weight. In the United States doctors are still allowed to prescribe synthetic THC to patients with poor appetites who need to gain weight.

Today, supplying cannabis without a prescription is illegal almost everywhere in the world, except in the Netherlands, where it can be legally consumed in special cafes. Marijuana has been approved for some uses in Canada and may be legally imported into Great Britain and Spain with prescriptions.

Cannabis Chart

At all consumption levels:

- behavioral effects may include euphoria; increased sensory perceptions; lowering of inhibitions; psychotic episodes; paranoia; and lack of motivation after long-term use.
- physical effects may include increased appetite and fatigue.
- withdrawal symptoms may include decreased appetite; insomnia; craving for marijuana.

Drug	Administered	Duration of Effects
Marijuana	oral, smoked	2–4 hours
Synthetic THC	oral, smoked	2–4 hours
Hashish	oral, smoked	2–4 hours

Depressants

Depressants are a major drug group made up of legal, illegal, or misused legal drugs that reduce brain signals to other parts of the body. Depressants slow down processes that direct breathing, heart rate, speech, large and small muscle movements, and thought processes, such as reaction time, alertness, and judgment. Drugs that slow down such

ALCOHOL AND CIGARETTES ARE LEGAL AND EASILY AVAILABLE. FOR THAT REASON, EXPERTS CONSIDER THEM GATEWAY DRUGS, THE FIRST ONES TEENS TRY WHEN THEY EXPERIMENT WITH PSYCHOACTIVE SUBSTANCES.

activities include anesthetics, such as GHB; anti-anxiety medications, such as Valium and Xanax; the hypnotic Rohypnol; the sedative Methaqualone (Quaaludes); sleeping pills; and barbiturates.

By far, the most widely used and abused depressant is legally available to anyone over twenty-one. That drug is alcohol. Many people tend to think of alcohol as a stimulant that makes people lively and happy. It does seem to have some stimulant properties at lower doses. Alcohol's depressive effects, however, kick in quickly with each additional drink. While a drinker may at first give the appearance of being lively and stimulated, with subsequent drinks, he or she will soon begin to slur words, walk unsteadily, and think unclearly. These outward behaviors indicate that signals between the brain and speech, memory, and motor centers are slowing down. Signals to areas of the brain that influence judgment and inhibitions that keep a person safe slow down as well.

Some of these same depressive effects are magnified when someone takes high doses of a depressant or combines one kind of depressant with another or with another kind of drug.

Depressant drugs, though not alcohol, are often tasteless, colorless, and odorless. Someone can easily add one to a drink without the victim's knowledge. He or she may become incapable of fending off an attack or even of remembering the assault. For that reason, these depressants are sometimes called club drugs, date rape drugs, or drug-assisted assault drugs. They are most often used for their general intoxicating effect. GHB and Rohypnol are two drugs in popular use since about the mid-1990s. To help stop such abuse, Congress passed the Drug-Induced Rape Prevention and Punishment Act in 1996. It includes harsh penalties against someone who uses a controlled substance to aid in a sexual assault.

Facts About Depressants

At overdose consumption levels:

- behavioral effects may include slurred speech, disorientation, unsteady gait, impaired memory.
- physical effects may include shallow breathing, weak and rapid pulse, coma, death.
- withdrawal symptoms may include anxiety, convulsions, insomnia, tremors, death.

Drug	How Taken	Effects last
Alcohol	Orally	1–3 hours
Barbiturates	Orally	12 hours
Benzodiazepines	Orally	1–8 hours
GHB	Orally	6 hours
Methaqualone	Orally	Up to 8 hours
Rohypnol	Orally	Up to 8 hours
Sedatives	Orally	Up to 8 hours

Hallucinogens, Dissociatives, and Deliriants

The three categories of hallucinogens—psychedelics, dissociatives, and deliriants—are made up of drugs that change feelings and perceptions of reality. They have been used for thousands of years in religious ceremonies and in more recent decades as recreational drugs to induce mind-expanding experiences.

For many people, hallucinogens mean LSD, the perception-altering psychedelic of the 1960s. It came into popular use after cult leader and Harvard professor Timothy Leary spoke in Golden Gate Park in San Francisco on the bliss of experiencing its effects. But Leary was wrong when he said the experience was not only exciting but harmless. The mind-distorting effects of these drugs are wildly unpredictable. The so-called "trip" may be pleasurable at one time and highly disturbing the next. A deep-seated depression may occur, causing people to act in bizarre ways that may threaten their lives.

Hallucinogens act on the brain when their chemicals cause the elevation of normal brain chemicals called neurotransmitters. These essential chemical compounds send signals between the brain's neurons, or nerve cells. When neurotransmitters build up, the brain may behave abnormally. One neurotransmitter, serotonin, affects behavior, mood, and sleep. A buildup of serotonin may be responsible for the strange and often frightening experiences that hallucinogen users have reported.

Long-term permanent brain damage has not been reported with hallucinogen use. However, the user may suffer from sweating, nausea, high blood pressure, and an elevated heart rate. Illegal perception-altering drugs, which produce a distorted sense of reality or an "out-of-body" feeling, include mescaline, Ecstasy, Ketamine, and forms of psilocybin mushroom. The disconnected feelings that such drugs induce may endanger a user's safety by impairing his or her objective judgment of reality. Because hallucinogens have sometimes caused users to engage in dangerous behaviors, deaths have been associated with the use of these drugs.

Hallucinogen Chart

At any consumption level:

- behavioral effects may include heightened awareness of stimuli; exaggerated sense of time and space; paranoia; inability to make judgments, remember events, or feel pain.
- physical effects may include drowsiness, heart problems, and elevated body temperature.
- withdrawal symptoms may include depression and craving for the drug.

Drug	Administered	Duration of Effects
LSD	oral, injected	8–12 hours
MDMA (Ecstasy)	oral, injected, snorted	4–6 hours
mescaline	oral	4–8 hours
PCP, Ketamine, Psilocybin mushrooms	oral, smoked, snorted, or injected	1–12 hours

Inhalants

The fumes from many household products, such as glue, paint removers, and cleaning aerosols, cigarette lighters, and gasoline, as well certain dental and medical products make up another category of dangerous psychoactive substances. Those who abuse inhalants do so by breathing the fumes of chemical substances into their lungs to achieve certain emotional and physical effects. Readily available household cleaning aerosols or solvents—liquids that dilute other substances—make it easy for curious children and preteens to experiment with toxic substances before they have adequate knowledge of their dangers.

A special class of inhalants are nitrites, commonly known as poppers, and used primarily as sexual enhancers. Most contain isobutyl nitrite or butyl nitrite and are sold in small brown bottles labelled as video head cleaner or leather cleaner.

Less available are medical and dental drugs that release fumes. Medicinally, these drugs are sometimes used to revive unconscious victims. However, some adults obtain these drugs illicitly to inhale them. One is nitrous oxide ("laughing gas"), used in some dental procedures. The other is amyl nitrate.

As with alcohol, inhalants slow down brain processes. However, since inhaling delivers drugs to the brain faster than any other method, effects kick in immediately. Inhalants are far more dangerous than alcohol because of their rapid delivery and their toxicity. These can cause brain, nerve, and major organ damage with a single use. Brain function can slow vital processes such as breathing and heartbeat so quickly that death occurs due to Sudden Sniffing Death Syndrome.

Inhalants Chart

At all consumption levels:

- behavioral effects may include memory impairment, slurred speech, and unsteady gait.
- physical effects may include dizziness; headache; nosebleed; slow breathing; irregular heartbeat; tissue damage in nose, throat, lungs, and major organs; nerve and brain damage; convulsions; coma; death.
- withdrawal symptoms may include anxiety, tremors, hallucinations, convulsions, dependency.

Drug	Administered	Duration of Effect
Amyl Nitrate	inhaled	1 minute
Nitrous Oxide	inhaled	30 seconds
Other inhalants	inhaled	1–3 minutes

Narcotics

The word narcotics is derived from a Greek word meaning "to make numb." They include the natural opiates morphine, heroin, opium, and codeine. They reduce pain but also cause drowsiness. All are made from plant substances in the opium poppy. Opium itself is made from the dried juice of the opium poppy. Codeine is found in opium in small amounts, and morphine is opium's chief ingredient. Opiate narcotics are illegal except for prescribed, controlled quantities of morphine and codeine. Thousands of tons of legal and illegal opiates are produced each year at drug factories around the world and in the United States. Most of Mexico's opium production—about 2 percent of the world market—is smuggled into the United States.

Opiates have a high dependency potential. According to a *Consumers Union* report in 1972, "a very serious shortcoming of the opiates in common use . . . is their brief period of action." A regular opiate user will eventually reach tolerance, that point where the dose must be increased to get the same desired effect. Withdrawal from the drug may result in physical pain and anxiety and a craving to get the drug to repeat the experience.

The narcotics' classification also includes powerful synthetic painkilling analgesics called opioids and hydrocodone. These produce some of the same effects as natural opiates. Opioids include the Oxycodone drugs Oxycontin, Percocet, and Percadone. Hydrocodone drugs include Vicodin, Lorcet, and Lortab, among others.

At prescribed levels and when used for a short term, all these narcotics are effective pain relievers. At unprescribed high doses and longer terms, opioids and hydrocodone drugs, like the opiates, have a strong potential for creating dependence. They not only reduce pain but also produce feelings of deep contentment when taken at unprescribed high levels. Some users begin to crave a repetition of those feelings and the drugs that produced them. They can dull a user's senses and induce sleep. At overdose levels, such narcotics can be fatal if the body becomes so sedated that its basic functioning stops. They are dangerous in combination with depressants, particularly alcohol, that also slow down the body's major functions.

Opiates, opioids, and hydrocodone drugs are quickly habit forming. Eventually, a regular user will reach tolerance, the point at which increasingly high doses must be taken to achieve the original intensity at a lower dose. Opiate and opioid withdrawal may result in physical pain and anxiety and a strong crav-

PRODUCTION OF OPIUM, FROM WHICH MORPHINE, HEROIN, AND CODEINE ARE MADE, BEGAN CENTURIES AGO IN ASIA. THESE SAME ILLICIT DRUGS, AND OTHERS, STILL COME TO THE WEST ALONG A DRUG SMUGGLING ROUTE THAT BEGINS IN BURMA, LAOS, AND THAILAND, CALLED THE GOLDEN TRIANGLE.

ing for the drug. Because of the dangers of abuse, opiates, opioids, and hydrocodone narcotics are tightly regulated.

Uncontrolled narcotics that are approved by the Food and Drug Administration in the United States are milder analgesics. Consumers can buy many effective ones—aspirin, ibuprofen, and acetaminophen, for example—over the counter to treat simple pain.

Narcotics Chart

At overdose consumption levels:

- behavioral effects may include drowsiness, euphoria, depressed breathing, slurred speech, disorientation, unsteady gait, impaired memory.
- physical effects may include shallow breathing, convulsions, coma, death.
- withdrawal symptoms may include anxiety, irritability, loss of appetite, tremors, panic, cramps, chills, sweating, convulsions, insomnia, tremors, death.

Drug	Administered	Duration of Effect
Codeine	oral, injected	3–6 hours
Heroin	injected, smoked, sniffed	3–6 hours
Morphine	injected, oral, smoked	4–5 hours
Opium	oral, smoked	3–7 hours
Oxycodone	oral, injected	3–12 hours

Stimulants

Stimulants, which increase alertness and energy, have been around for a long time. In World War II, soldiers took stimulants to combat exhaustion on the battle-field. They helped asthmatics and those with other respiratory problems to breathe more easily. They have been prescribed to treat narcolepsy, a sleeping disorder that causes someone to fall asleep almost anywhere at any time. Stimulants are sometimes used as well to treat depression that has not responded to other drugs.

Caffeine is a well-known stimulant, usually con-sumed in safe doses. Some of the more potent stimulants—cocaine and amphetamines, for example—make the user feel exhilarated and energetic. The nicotine in cigarettes also produces some of these feelings. Because of these effects, all stimulants have abuse potential, including those that are medically prescribed.

Doctors prescribe Ritalin, for example, to treat narcolepsy as well as attention deficit hyperactivity disorder (ADHD) in children. Paradoxically, Ritalin has a stabilizing effect on the hyperactive behavior of children with ADHD but a stimulating effect on non-ADHD users who use Ritalin illicitly. Such users, including some high school and college students, obtain Ritalin pills illegally. They take the pills orally or grind them into a powder that they inject or snort to achieve the effect of exhilaration and heightened energy levels.

Stimulant Chart

At overdose or unprescribed consumption levels:

- behavioral effects may include agitation, euphoria, insomnia, and loss of appetite, but a lessening of agitation in users with ADHD.
- physical effects may include increased blood pressure and pulse, hallucinations, elevated body temperature, convulsions, and death.
- withdrawal symptoms may include excessive sleepiness, disorientation, depression.

Drug	Administered	Duration of Effect
Amphetamines	oral, injected	2–4 hours
Cocaine	oral, injected	1–2 hours
Methamphetamine	oral, injected	2–4 hours
	inhaled, smoked	16 hours
Ritalin	oral	2–4 hours

Drugs from A to Z describes the most commonly misused drugs, from alcohol and marijuana to stimulants, such as nicotine and cocaine. Each entry lists the drug's type, its chemical makeup, the ways in which it is used and abused, and the physical and emotional effects on the user of the drug. For easy reference, drugs are listed alphabetically.

CONSUMERS OF PRESCRIBED DRUGS CAN FIND ANSWERS TO MANY QUESTIONS ABOUT PARTICULAR DRUGS FROM THEIR DOCTORS, PHARMACISTS, ON WEB SITES, AND IN THE INFORMATION SHEETS THAT COME WITH THE DRUG. THAT IS NOT TRUE FOR UNPRESCRIBED LEGAL DRUGS OR ILLICIT DRUGS.

2 FROM ALCOHOL TO CODEINE

Many first-time, experimental, and experienced drug users sample their first drugs before they ever ask tough questions about these substances. While drug-prevention programs in the schools attempt to educate young people about the dangers of certain drugs, some drug takers experiment before they fully understand the information. Research shows that people who go on to abuse drugs later in life are usually those who started drug use earliest in life. The drugs that the youngest users first try are fairly easy to get—inhalants, alcohol, and cigarettes. Their very familiarity and availability often keep potential users from realizing their dangers. All of them can lead to dependence, health problems, and accidents. Their early use often paves the way to future use of completely illegal drugs.

The best time for anyone to get information and the answers to questions about the negative effects of taking drugs is before that person takes the first sniff or the first sip of a psychoactive drug. The latest research provides some of those answers. Early and regular alcohol use impairs new memory formation in preteens and teens. Early and regular teen smokers who think they will be able to quit smoking later on probably won't. And early and habitual teen marijuana users may have a tough time finding the motivation to complete the tasks of adolescence—building relationships, getting an education, making plans for the future.

Alcohol

No one knows when alcohol was first used, but the Egyptians certainly drank wine as early as 4000 BCE. They even had a god of wine, Osiris, also said to have invented beer, an important beverage in Egyptian everyday life. Intoxication from over imbibing also occurred since there were warnings against taking in too much.

Throughout history, societies have warned about the dangers of alcohol. Recognizing that alcoholism harmed families and workers, most societies created laws to control or prohibit it completely. The United States government outlawed the manufacture and consumption of alcohol by passing the Eighteenth Amendment to the Constitution in 1920. That amendment launched the era known as Prohibition. During that period, people could not buy alcohol legally except by doctor's prescription. As with illegal drug-making today, Prohibition fostered the growth of black markets where illegal sales of alcohol took place behind closed doors. Speakeasies, the secret clubs where patrons could purchase and drink alcohol illegally, sprouted up in most major cities. Illegal alcohol sales sometimes led to the corruption of law enforcement officials who were tempted with bribes to look the other way.

Because the profits of making and selling illegal alcohol were so great, the prohibition of it gave rise to gangs and organized crime families that made and distributed alcohol illegally. In the end, Prohibition did not stop alcohol consumption. Moreover, it had the unintended consequence of fostering crime. Recognizing the law's failure in accomplishing its original goals, the government ended Prohibition in 1933.

Alcohol itself is a natural, colorless liquid produced by fermenting certain carbohydrates from fruits and grains. The alcohol found in alcoholic beverages, wine, and beer occurs when yeast spores cause sugar to ferment, resulting in ethyl alcohol or ethanol. Other non-beverage alcohols, such as methanol, or wood alcohol, are used to make plastics and varnishes. Propanol is used in cosmetics and rubbing alcohol.

Alcohol use is so common that most people do not regard it as a depressant with serious consequences for heavy drinkers. However, many social

ALCOHOL DEPRESSES AND SLOWS DOWN BRAIN FUNCTIONS INVOLVED IN REACTION TIME AND JUDGMENT, THE TWO MAIN SKILLS NEEDED TO DRIVE A CAR SAFELY.

drinkers manage alcohol consumption responsibly. They drink moderately and do not drink and drive. Many people drink with meals only. As a result they consume less alcohol than does someone who drinks on an empty stomach. Food slows down alcohol's intoxicating effects on the body. Whether alcohol is taken with food or without it, its molecules eventually pass into the bloodstream and travel throughout the body. A drinker's size and weight, quantity of alcohol consumed, as well the presence or absence of food in the stomach, all affect a person's reaction to alcohol. Females generally feel the effects of alcohol more quickly than males do. This is due to the fact that female organs and circulatory systems are generally smaller than those in males. The alcohol has smaller spaces in which to travel through the body.

Unlike moderate drinkers, those who drink too often and to excess may face damaging physical effects. Recent studies have shown that alcohol consumption at a young age may permanently and adversely affect adolescent brain development in the hippocampus area where new memories are formed. As with many drugs, regular alcohol consumption can lead to dependence—alcoholism. Research shows that underage drinkers who have their first drink before age fifteen are five times more likely to become alcoholics than those who begin drinking later.

With dependence can come damage to various body organs. Cirrhosis of the liver is fairly common in older drinkers who have abused alcohol for many years. This irreversible liver damage results in scarring of the liver until it no longer functions; it is a fatal condition.

Heavy drinkers who also smoke are susceptible to deadly cancers of the mouth and throat. Combinations of alcohol and other drugs can prove fatal. As a depressant, alcohol slows down major physical and mental processes. It can dull the senses,

Facts on Teens and Alcohol Abuse

- Average age when teens try alcohol: eleven years old for boys and thirteen years old for girls.

- Alcoholic teens: an estimated three million in the United States.

- People at risk for alcohol abuse: family history of abuse, depression, low self-esteem; a feeling that they "don't fit in"; lack of parental support and communication; tendency for risk-taking, impulsive behavior.

- Hazards of abuse: car crashes, the leading cause of death among those fifteen to twenty-four years old; risk for alcoholism due to early onset of drinking.

- Suicide: third leading cause of death for those from eighteen to twenty-five years old.

- High-risk sex: alcohol may contribute to uninhibited sexual behavior.

compromise memory, and impair a user's judgment and driving ability. Alcohol is often also a contributing factor in deaths from drug overdose. At overdose levels, such as the kind that take place during a drinking binge, alcohol can slow down the breathing rate to the point of inducing a coma and possibly death. In combination, alcohol and heroin or alcohol and opiates and opioids can also shut down respiration completely. Excess alcohol may result in pulmonary edema, when the user drowns in vomit.

In 2005, underage drinkers between the ages of twelve and twenty accounted for 142,000 emergency room visits due to problems related to their drinking. Alcohol-related automobile crashes and firearm accidents cause the deaths of thousands of young people.

NICD Classification of Alcohol: *Depressant* with some stimulating effects at low doses

Scientific name: The word alcohol is from *al kohl,* an Arabic phrase initially referring to any finely ground material and later to the spirit or essence of wine.

Street names: Booze, Suds, in addition to hundreds of others

How obtained: Users over twenty-one may purchase alcohol legally in most places in the United States.

Medical uses: Some studies show that red wine consumption may help to prevent heart disease. Alcohol can also be used as a disinfectant to kill germs.

Illicit uses: Underage drinking to experience alcohol's effects; binge drinking; drinking and driving.

How taken: Swallowed, either by itself or in various mixtures with other beverages, such as water, seltzer, and juices.

How alcohol works: When someone drinks alcohol, molecules of its active ingredient, ethanol, enter the small intestine and are absorbed into the bloodstream. These molecules are small enough to pass through the blood-brain barrier, which normally prevents many harmful substances from entering the brain. Once in the brain, alcohol's ethanol molecules activate GABA (gamma-aminobutryic acid). This neurotransmitter is responsible for slowing down normal brain processes, such as thinking, moving, speaking, and digesting food. The effects are slower thinking; more uncoordinated physical movements as orders from the brain to the muscles slow down; poorer short-term memory storage; impaired judgment; and nausea.

Interaction: Alcohol can increase the effects of many medications. It should never be taken without first reading warnings about alcohol tolerance with the other drug. Alcohol is particularly dangerous in combination with other depressants.

Dependence potential: Regular and heavy alcohol use may lead to dependence, alcoholism characterized by a craving for alcohol despite negative physical, social, and emotional consequences.

Social dangers: An intoxicated person frequently relaxes inhibitions and behaves in unusual and sometimes inappropriate ways. Drunk drivers cause hundreds of thousands of injuries and tens of thousands of deaths each year.

Legal dangers: Although it is legal for adults to drink alcohol, they may get into trouble with the law when alcohol impairs their driving ability enough to cause a car crash. Those under twenty-one are not allowed to buy or consume alcoholic beverages in the United States.

Use and withdrawal symptoms: When alcohol use is stopped after overuse, the habitual drinker may experience sweating, vomiting, irritability, difficulty sleeping, the shakes, and sometimes *delirium tremors*—called the DTs.

Amphetamines

Amphetamines and cocaine are the two most widely abused stimulants. Because amphetamines improve an individual's alertness, they can relieve the symptoms of fatigue in people who suffer from a sleep disorder called narcolepsy. Amphetamines are also used to treat attention deficit hyperactivity disorder (ADHD). However, when used in unprescribed ways and dosages, amphetamines increase heart rate and blood pressure. They can cause anxiety, sleeplessness, blurred vision, and can lead to physical collapse.

NICD Classification of Amphetamines: *Stimulant*

Scientific name: Amphetamines (e.g., Benzedrine, Dextroamphetamine)

Street names: Black Beauties, Bennies, Greenies, Speed, Uppers, Whiz

How obtained: By prescription from doctor or pharmacist for some conditions. Some "lookalike" drugs are produced in illicit laboratories, but potency varies from batch to batch.

Medical uses: To increase alertness in patients with sleeping disorders, such as narcolepsy; to relieve breathing disorders; to treat ADHD.

Illicit uses: To stay awake, increase strength, become more alert, lose weight, experience euphoria.

How taken: Orally; injected; pill form; or reduced to crystals that are snorted or injected. In any form, amphetamines are a powerful stimulant on the central nervous system.

How stimulants work: Powerful stimulants of the central nervous system, amphetamines block transporters of dopamine, a neurotransmitter in the brain's pleasure circuit. Dopamine then accumulates in higher-than-normal levels, producing feelings of alertness, euphoria, and increased energy, as well as increased heart rate and blood pressure. At unprescribed, unregulated levels, symptoms may include nausea, jitteriness, and irritability. Overdose can lead to heart failure, convulsions, paranoia, bizarre behavior, or death.

Interaction: Amphetamines should not be used with insulin or antidepressant drugs and may cause heart palpitations, high blood pressure, and other heart symptoms.

Dependence potential: High potential for dependence as user turns to amphetamines to avoid letdown feelings of depression when the drug wears off. Dependence may lead to larger doses or stronger drugs, such as cocaine, to maintain the "high."

Social dangers: Dizziness associated with overdose levels may incapacitate a user for a time.

Legal dangers: The misuse of prescription drugs is illegal.

Use and withdrawal symptoms: Depression, sleeplessness, irritability.

Anabolic steroids

The human body produces two main types of steroids. The adrenal steroids on top of the kidneys control such processes as the response to stress. The other main steroid types include the sex hormones. Estrogen and progesterone are the female sex hormones. Androgen and testosterone are the male sex hormones.

Anabolic steroids are manufactured variations of the male sex hormones and are developed to increase body mass and improve muscle tissue. Anabolic refers to the chemical reactions in the body that build up tissue. Legal anabolic steroids are available as prescription drugs to treat chronic wasting conditions such as AIDS and cancer or delayed growth problems in children. Because steroids build muscles, they help to improve performance in sports.

Anabolic steroids came into more general use in the 1950s when Soviet Olympic teams began giving their members steroids to increase muscle power. The treatments worked, and the Soviets dominated the Olympics in strength performance during that period. In fact, some of the Russian women took so many steroids that they had to undergo chromosome tests to make sure they really were women. After that, some Olympic participants—United States athletes included—began to build an anabolic steroid program. Professional athletes began steroid use, especially baseball and football players. Before long, seemingly amazing records were set, such as Mark McGwire's seventy home runs in 1998, which beat Roger Maris's sixty-one home runs in 1961, which beat Babe Ruth's sixty home runs in 1927. These record breakers began to be questioned. In 2001, Barry Bonds hit seventy-three home runs, but he denies taking anabolic steroids. However, sports organizations are working to ban the use of anabolic steroids in all competitive sports.

Anabolic steroids are also being abused by some adolescents, college-age students, and young adults. In *When Winning Costs Too Much,* the authors report that "teens feel pressure to take steroids, and they believe the drugs are easily available." Moreover, they generally enhance one's physical appearance. For all these reasons, steroid use is on the increase, especially among teenage boys. However, unprescribed use of these hormones can have many negative effects on the body and mind.

NICD Classification of Anabolic Steroids:
Anabolic Steroid
Scientific name: Anabolic-androgenic steroids
Street names: Hype, Juice, Rocket fuel, Roids
How obtained: Doctors legally prescribe ana-bolic steroids to treat certain medical conditions. Illicit users obtain them from sellers who purchase them from laboratories outside the United States

Anabolic Steroid Chart

At overdose or unprescribed consumption levels:

- behavioral effects may include anger and aggressive behavior.

- physical effects may include acne; abnormal development of male breast tissue; shrinking of testicles.

- withdrawal symptoms may include depression.

Drug	Administered	Duration of Effects
Testosterone	injected	2–4 weeks
Parabolan	injected	varies

where the drug is legal. Other users get them as veterinary products within the United States.

Medical uses: Doctors prescribe anabolic steroids to stimulate growth in cases of growth failure; to induce puberty in young men when it is delayed; to improve appetite; and to increase red blood cells in anemia, though other drugs are replacing anabolic steroids for this purpose.

Illicit use: Some users, particularly young male athletes, take unprescribed, often unsafe doses of anabolic steroids to build muscle and improve athletic performance or overall physical attractiveness.

How taken: Orally; injected into the muscle; or rubbed on the skin. Some users employ stacking,

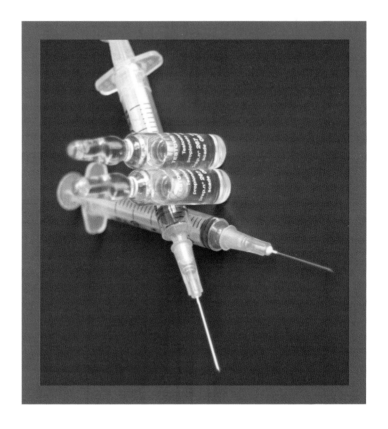

ANABOLIC STEROIDS HAVE BEEN IN USE SINCE THE 1930S, WHEN DOCTORS PRESCRIBED THEM FOR ANEMIA AND MALNUTRITION AND LATER TO STIMULATE APPETITE AND BONE GROWTH. SOME ADULT ATHLETES AND TEENS MISUSE ANABOLIC STEROIDS TO BUILD MUSCLE AND IMPROVE ATHLETIC PERFORMANCE.

which means using two or more kinds of steroids at once in the belief that this will speed up the building process. Abusers also pyramid by starting with a low dose of one steroid and increasing the dose for up to twelve weeks. They then decrease usage for

46

another twelve weeks until they are down to zero. This is all done to enhance the muscle and tissue building process, although there is no scientific evidence that pyramiding works.

How anabolic steroids work: The body naturally produces steroids, the hormones that promote growth and the development of sexual characteristics. The synthetic anabolic steroids mimic some of these natural processes and disrupt others. Artificial steroids bind to muscle receptors for androgen, a major male sex hormone, which in turn affects the body's normal protein production. Anabolic steroids also block some of the effects of cortisol, a stress hormone. The result of altered protein production, combined with the reduced effects of cortisol, helps to increase red blood cell production, bone growth, muscle mass, and appetite.

Dependence potential: Some athletes taking anabolic steroids regularly become preoccupied with continuing to use the drugs to build their muscles. They may experience depression when they stop taking them.

Social dangers: Consumption of unregulated, unprescribed high doses of anabolic steroids is associated with mood swings, irritability, and aggressiveness.

Legal dangers: Steroid use is illegal in most professional and high school sports.

Use and withdrawal symptoms: In males, high doses of anabolic steroids do build muscle mass but also may shrink testes and cause abnormal growth of male breast tissue. Other physical effects may include liver tumors and jaundice. The smaller numbers of women who take anabolic steroids may experience increased growth of body hair but loss of hair on their heads. They may develop a deeper voice. High blood pressure and cancer are some of the dangers of long-term steroid use. Steroids may build up cholesterol in the body. Men have an increased risk of prostate cancer and infertility. Abuse can cause heart attack, stroke, and liver problems after long-term use.

Benzodiazepines
Benzodiazepines are drugs that depress, or slow down, the central nervous system to give users a feeling of calm, relaxation, or sleepiness. Widely prescribed, benzodiazepines are commonly known as tranquilizers and sleeping pills. The first benzodiazepine was discovered almost accidentally in 1954 by an Austrian scientist working for Hoffmann-La Roche pharmaceutical company. Further research found it to be an effective tranquilizer.

NICD Classification of Benzodiazepines: *Depressant*
Scientific name: Well-known benzodiazepines and their trade names include: Alprazolam (Xanax),

Diazepam (Valium), Lorazepam (Ativan), Clonazepam (Klonopin), and Flunitrazepam (Rohypnol).

Street name: Commonly called Benzos.

Medical uses: Benzodiazepines are used for treating anxiety, insomnia, muscle spasms, seizures, alcohol dependency, and common physical conditions such as chronic arthritis pain, high blood pressure, and skin problems. They are sometimes used to relax a patient during certain medical procedures, such as dental work. However, most benzodiazepines are prescribed to reduce anxiety and stress; to relieve common medical problems; to promote sleep; and as an anesthetic before chemotherapy or some surgeries.

Illicit uses: Some benzodiazepines, such as GHB and Rohypnol, have been used as date rape drugs. Other drug users obtain unprescribed Xanax and Valium and use them to relax.

How obtained: Nearly all benzodiazepines are classified under Schedule IV of the Federal Controlled Substances Act, meaning the drug has recognized medical uses with low potential for overdose or misuse.

How taken: Most benzodiazepines are taken orally, although they can be administered intravenously, intramuscularly, or as a suppository.

How benzodiazepines work: The drug enters the bloodstream and reaches the brain, where it acts on the brain's chief neurotransmitter, GABA, to subdue cells in the central nervous system. By increasing the efficiency of GABA, the drug slows down brain activity, resulting in a sedating effect. However, at unprescribed overdose levels, or in combination with other depressant drugs—alcohol, for example—benzodiazepines can slow heart rate so much that sufficient oxygen fails to reach the brain. Coma or death may result.

Dependence potential: If taken daily during a period longer than a few days, benzodiazepines have potential for causing dependency.

Interaction: These drugs should not be taken with alcohol, which may lead to coma when brain function becomes severely depressed. Combining benzodiazepines with pain relievers can sometimes also lead to coma.

Legal dangers: Flunitrazepam (Rohypnol), despite being a Schedule IV benzodiazepine, is not available legally in the United States. First-offense for simple possession is a felony.

Use and withdrawal symptoms: Long-term use of benzodiazepines can worsen depression and cause sleeplessness. Withdrawal may be erratic, with some days free of symptoms while at other times users may feel ill or distressed. Most users recover completely. Withdrawal symptoms can include anxiety, breathing difficulties, dizziness, heart palpitations, and indigestion. However, abruptly stopping the drug can produce unpleasant withdrawal symptoms, such as delusions and con-vulsions. An overdose, especially combined with alcohol, can lead to coma.

Cocaine

Cocaine, one of the oldest known drugs, is a powerful addictive stimulant that directly affects the brain. Coca leaves, the source of cocaine, have been ingested for thousands of years. Native tribes in the Andes ranges of South America chewed leaves of the coca plant to boost energy in the high-altitude, thin-air climate. They also found that chewing the coca leaves took away a toothache. The energy boost came from cocaine alkaloid, a chemical agent in the leaves. Chewing coca leaves became a common habit. However, since the drug was rarely taken in large quantities, few realized that it was addictive.

By the late 1800s, doctors were recommending cocaine to treat a variety of conditions, such as asthma, depression, and aches and pains. Into the 1900s, people could buy cocaine as an elixir that could cure everything from a sore throat to a broken heart.

Today, cocaine is an illegal drug in every state, yet it is widely abused. Although the rates of overall cocaine use have decreased somewhat in the last decade, consumption is rising somewhat again among teenagers and college students. In 2004, an estimated two million Americans abused cocaine.

An extremely potent freebase form of cocaine is called crack. The powdered cocaine hydrochloride form is processed to a smokeable substance. The street name refers to the crackling sound made when the mixture is smoked. Inhaled, crack affects the brain within seconds as compared to the fifteen minutes or so when cocaine is snorted. A dose of crack is also cheaper than cocaine in powder form. A single crack "rock" costs from ten to twenty dollars, whereas a single dose of cocaine powder to snort runs from eighty to one hundred fifty dollars. That makes crack highly affordable on the streets of many neighborhoods.

NICD Classification of Cocaine: *Stimulant*

Scientific name: Erythroxylon coca, bush grown primarily in South America

Street names: Crack, Coke, Rock, Snow, among many others

Medical uses: There is some limited medical use of cocaine hydrochloride as a topical anesthetic to numb the interior of the mouth or nose.

Illicit uses: Cocaine users mainly use the drug illegally as a recreational drug to experience its euphoric effects.

How taken: When chewed or eaten, the coca leaves are mixed with an acidic substance, such as lime juice, then chewed into a wad, put between mouth and gums, and sucked of juices. The most common method of cocaine consumption is snorting or sniffing fine particles of cocaine powder. Cocaine is sometimes smoked via a glass tube. Occasionally, cocaine powder is rubbed along the gum line. The injection of cocaine and heroin in a combination called a Speedball has killed people.

How obtained: Most cocaine is grown in South America and smuggled into the United States. It is broken down into smaller loads before it is smuggled across the border. The many smuggling techniques include airdrops, ships, and commercial fishing vessels. The drug reaches the streets where, in many areas, organized gangs operate the cocaine trade on a large scale and sell the drug to street buyers or to customers by appointment.

How cocaine works: Cocaine is a fast-acting drug that is absorbed quickly. Whether eaten, chewed, snorted, or inhaled, cocaine enters the bloodstream and affects the central nervous system. There its molecules reach the key part of the brain, called the ventral tegmental area (VTA), which is part of the brain's pleasure circuit and involved in rewarding stimuli. Cocaine blocks DAT, the dopamine transporter protein. As a result, dopamine, a pleasure-enhancing neurotransmitter; accumulates. Short-term effects, which are felt almost immediately, include euphoria, energy, and mental alertness. The drug may lessen the need for food or sleep.

Negative long-term effects of cocaine include craving, as users try to experience the pleasure and intensity of their first high. Other negative effects include paranoia, restlessness, irritability, even full-blown psychosis where the person loses touch with reality. There is danger of contacting HIV/AIDS and hepatitis from sharing needles or other paraphernalia when cocaine users inject the drug. Medical complications include respiratory problems and heart failure, strokes, seizures, and gastrointestinal troubles.

Dependence potential: Cocaine/crack consumption rapidly creates dependence due to its fast-acting properties. Cocaine consumption causes changes in the brain's pleasure circuit and distribution of dopamine. The user craves more frequent and stronger doses. This expensive habit can take over one's life. Continuous sniffing can destroy the nasal passages or cause the nasal septum to collapse entirely. A regular cocaine user may forget to eat or to maintain healthy habits. Such neglect may lead to many physical problems. Symptoms of withdrawal include general bad feelings and panic.

Interaction: Cocaine can be lethal, especially if injected with heroin.

Social dangers: The drug craving regular cocaine users experience causes many of them to ruin relationships, jobs, finances, and forget future goals in pursuit of the drug.

Legal dangers: Cocaine has been considered a "hard drug" in the United States since 1914. The production, distribution, and sale of cocaine and its products are illegal.

Use and withdrawal symptoms: Recovery from cocaine dependence is a long-term process and commitment. Drug counselors often recommend group sessions for many months of therapy. Doctors sometimes prescribe medications such as antidepressants to help the cocaine abuser cope with depressive symptoms and withdrawal.

Codeine

Codeine, which is found in small concentrations in opium, is available only by prescription in the United States. It is the most widely used, naturally occurring narcotic in medical treatment all over the world. In some states, codeine is available over-the-counter in small doses contained in some products. It is more commonly marketed in continental Europe and other regions than in the United States. Mainly a pain reliever, codeine is sometimes used to combat diarrhea and coughing. Of all the opiates, codeine is the weakest, yet still has strong opiate effects.

NICD Classification of Codeine:

Narcotic anesthetic
Scientific name: $C_{18}H_{21}NO_3$
Street names: Captain Cody, China white, Schoolboy
How obtained: Doctors may legally prescribe codeine to patients who need it as a pain reliever or cough suppressant. Some over-the-counter medications contain small quantities of codeine.
Medical uses: Mainly as a prescribed pain and cough reliever.
Illicit uses: Recreational for relaxation.

DRUG TAKING OFTEN REPLACES HEALTHY BEHAVIORS, SUCH AS EXERCISING, GETTING REGULAR SLEEP, AND EATING PROPERLY.

How taken: Codeine is usually swallowed or injected.

How codeine works: Codeine, whether swallowed or injected, relieves pain by blocking the pain signals that the brain sends to affected areas of the body. Codeine mimics endorphins, which are the naturally occurring painkilling chemicals that the human body produces. About thirty minutes after a dose, codeine inhibits the pain signals that the brain sends throughout the central nervous system. This occurs even though the source of the pain remains. The gastrointestinal tract readily absorbs the drug, and the bloodstream quickly carries it throughout the body.

Dependency potential: Codeine is habit forming and should only be used for legally prescribed purposes.

Interaction: Users should avoid alcohol or any other drugs with sedative effects when taking codeine as it greatly increases drowsiness and dizziness. Such combinations may severely depress respiration and heartbeat to the point of coma or death.

Social dangers: Recreational codeine use affects judgment in social situations.

Legal dangers: In the United States, codeine is legal only by prescription.

Use and withdrawal symptoms: Side effects include nausea, vomiting, dry mouth, constipation, and drowsiness. Prolonged use may cause respiratory problems as the body becomes accustomed to codeine and its cough-suppressing effects. Tolerance for the drug may develop. Users may also note a decreased sex drive.

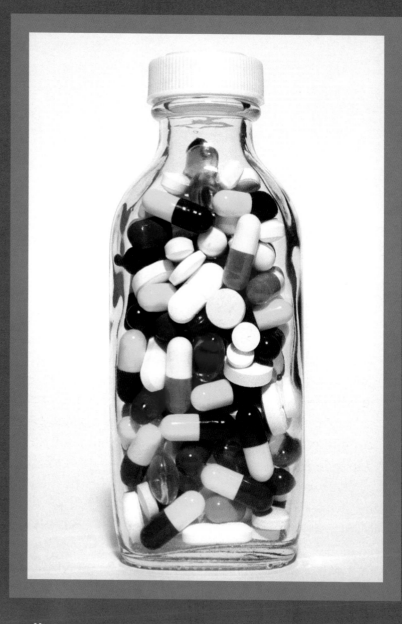

USERS WHO MIX DRUGS RISK DEADLY CONSEQUENCES BECAUSE COMBINED
DRUGS ENHANCE THE EFFECTS OF EACH DRUG IN UNPREDICTABLE WAYS.

3 FROM ECSTASY TO LSD

Many illicit drugs once began as legal, prescribed medications. Heroin was long used as a legitimate painkiller. Morphine and codeine, for example, are legal if prescribed for pain relief or coughing. Unprescribed, illicit use can lead to dependency.

The ways in which a drug is taken, rather than its medical advantages, determine whether a drug is being used in a safe, legally prescribed way or illicitly. GHB has been used as a legitimate treatment for insomnia—and misused as a date rape drug. Ketamine began as a veterinary product to anesthesize animals for various medical procedures and remains so. Yet it has also become popular among drug-taking clubgoers for its hallucinogenic effects. When a drug is taken in unprescribed ways, overdose, contamination, allergic reaction, or harmful interaction with other drugs are all dangerous possibilities.

Ecstasy (MDMA)
Ecstasy is a drug that can make the user feel "ecstatic" and energetic. To borrow a line from *My Fair Lady*, the Ecstasy user may well be able to "dance all night," which some Ecstasy users do after taking this "club" drug. Ecstasy simultaneously produces energy and a great wave of peacefulness and well being. Illicit users began to take Ecstasy as a dance club drug beginning in the 1960s. However, in higher doses, the user may be able to dance all night but also might not be able to halt a sexual assault. Because of its damaging effects, the drug has been illegal since 1985.

The drug has other serious physical effects. It increases heart rate and blood pressure. Effects may include anxiety, panic, and depression. Some researchers have found that Ecstasy can cause permanent brain damage. Ecstasy, like heroin and crack, is available on the streets. Fines are stiff for its sale and possession, but there are still many users who feel the high it produces is worth the risk of breaking the law.

NICD Classification of Ecstasy (MDMA): *Hallucinogen*
Scientific name: 3,4-methylenedioxymetham-

phetamine MDMA

Street names: Biscuits, Club Drugs, E, Ecstasy, Hug Drugs, M&Ms, Rhapsody

How obtained: Ecstasy is illegal.

Medical uses: There are no medical uses for Ecstasy, though it was first produced in Germany in 1912 as a possible appetite suppressant.

Illicit use: All Ecstasy use in the United States is illegal. Recreational users take it for multiple purposes: to ease anxiety, to reach a state of euphoria, and to remain in this state for long periods of time since Ecstasy blocks sensations of fatigue, thirst, and hunger.

How taken: Ecstasy is swallowed in tablet or capsule form.

How Ecstasy works: After a user swallows an Ecstasy tablet or capsule, the drug is absorbed into the bloodstream. When it reaches the brain, the drug blocks the uptake of an important chemical, serotonin, which then accumulates in the brain. Serotonin is responsible for mood swings and changes in perception. The excess serotonin heightens sensual awareness, euphoria, emotional energy, and strong positive feelings.

Ecstasy also reduces inhibitions. Negative effects may include nausea, severe sweating, blurred vision, depression, and higher blood pressure. There is some indication that heavy Ecstasy use may result in memory loss, although the exact nature of Ecstasy's effects on the human brain are not yet confirmed.

Interaction: Alcohol decreases the effects of Ecstasy. The drug can interfere with other drugs, such as cocaine or marijuana, resulting in sleep disturbances or aggressive behavior.

Dependency potential: Users may experience positive effects within an hour of taking a dose. The drug produces changes in mental abilities that can last up to a week or longer, making it dangerous to drive a car, for instance. Severe depression may follow.

Social dangers: Hallucinogens such as Ecstasy are associated with so-called rape drugs or rave drugs. Users may lose the inhibitions they might normally have about deciding to engage in sex.

Legal dangers: Ecstasy is illegal.

Use and withdrawal symptoms: Withdrawing from hallucinogen use does not seem to produce the cravings that occur with other habit-forming drugs. The dose level taken by a user tends to remain constant. Actually, because the hallucinogen experience itself is generally exhausting, users often do not take the drug more than once or twice a month. The effects experienced with a dose last for hours. There is a risk, however, of developing psychological problems, such as a mental breakdown that may require psychiatric treatment.

GHB (gamma-hydroxybutyrate)

Technically, GHB is a depressant and is better known as a date rape drug. It is naturally present in the body in very small amounts in the central nervous system as well as in the heart, kidneys, liver, and bones. As a drug, it is most commonly used in the form of a salt. It was sold in health food stores in the 1980s as a nutrient until so many health problems surfaced that the Food and Drug Administration (FDA) took it off the market.

NICD Classification of GHB: *Depressant*
Scientific name: Gamma-hydroxybutyrate
Street names: Cherry meth, G, Goop, Grievous Bodily Harm, Liquid X, Salty Water, Soap, Scoop
Medical uses: GHB is used as a general anesthetic and in the treatment of insomnia in some countries. In Italy, it is used in the treatment of alcoholism. Although it was banned in the United States in 1990, in 2002 it was approved for use under the trade name Xyrem to treat the sleep disorder known as narcolepsy.
Illicit uses: Recreational use to induce feelings of happiness, sensuality, and relaxation at lower doses. At higher doses it has been used in date-rape assaults.
How taken: As a colorless, odorless liquid GHB is usually swallowed. When combined with other liquids, even water, the saltiness is masked. It is often sold in small size bottles in concentrated form. A capful is enough for the desired effect.
How obtained: Except for treating sleeping disorders, GHB is banned in the United States.

How GHB works: The precise way in which GHB works in the body is not clear. Liquid GHB is swallowed and enters the bloodstream. Its molecules get into the brain, where it is believed to act as a neurotransmitter. It is similar to gamma-aminobutyric acid (GABA), the neurotransmitter that slows down brain signals to the rest of the body.

Dependence potential: Regular GHB use can cause physical and emotional dependence when taken on an intense and regular basis—every few hours for days or weeks at a time.

Interaction: Combining GHB with other drugs can bring on seizures.

Social dangers: GHB is known as a date-rape drug because the victim may be rendered incapable of fending off a sexual assault.

Legal dangers: GHB is generally illegal in the United States; selling and possession are subject to stiff fines and/or jail time.

Use and withdrawal symptoms: A GHB dose may render the user unconscious; this is called "scooping out" or "throwing down." Withdrawal effects include hallucinations, tremors, anxiety, chest pain, muscle and bone aches, and mental impairment. An overdose can bring on several hours of deep sleep from which it is difficult to awaken. There have been some reports of deaths from GHB overdose, although the extent of this danger is not certain. So far there is no firm data that shows extended GHB use damages the body organs.

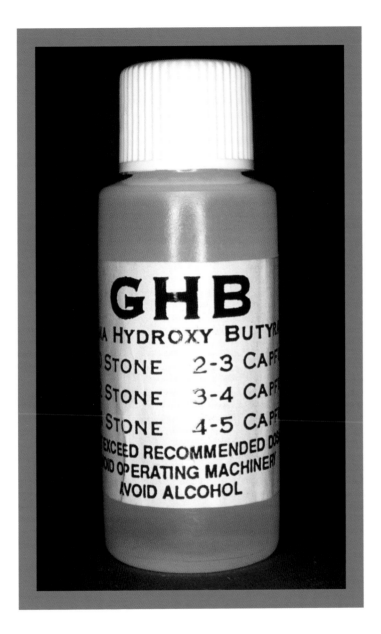

RESEARCHERS DEVELOPED GHB AND ROHYPNOL TO SEDATE PATIENTS BEFORE SURGERY AND OTHER MEDICAL PROCEDURES. BOTH HAVE SINCE BECOME DRUGS OF ABUSE AS CLUB DRUGS AND OCCASIONALLY AS DATE-RAPE DRUGS.

Heroin

Older drugs such as pure opium, pale in their potency when compared with heroin, made from the processed morphine of the opium poppy. German scientist Heinrich Dreser of Bayer Company developed heroin in the late 1800s. He named the crystalline powder heroin from the German word for "heroic." For over a century, it was used to relieve pain and to cure coughing. However, in the twentieth century, medicinal morphine, which is also derived from poppies, largely replaced medicinal heroin, which became illegal to sell or use.

Illicit uses of heroin, unfortunately, continue. Today's heroin is a potent drug. According to a *Consumers Union* report in 1972, a person who smoked opium a hundred years ago actually inhaled the vapor of a weak opium type containing less than 9 percent morphine. It would take about 400 grains of opium from that era to equal a single grain of today's injected heroin.

With a strong dependency potential, heroin can be a killer at first use. It is dangerous and expensive—addicts spend about fifteen thousand dollars a year for the drug—and illegal. Withdrawal symptoms can be intense and extremely painful. Yet, many drug users crave the drug and cannot kick the habit without intervention. Heroin gives the user a sudden and powerful sense of intense pleasure and well-being called a rush or a high. That experience keeps users going back, despite the real physical pain that may follow or the damage that may occur to the body and mind—and wallet.

Once hooked, a heroin user's life changes completely. His or her primary purpose in life is seeking and obtaining the drug. That quest comes before family, friends, work, and future goals. With continued use, the addict develops medical problems—collapsed veins from injections; infections of the heart valves; liver and kidney disease; and many types of respiratory problems. Needle sharing among heroin users can lead to hepatitis and HIV infections. Drug abusers often contract blood-borne viruses that they then pass on to their sexual partners and/or children.

Studies indicate heroin use is on the decline in the United States. However, most first-time users try it between the ages of eighteen and twenty-one when brain development is incomplete. At these young ages, the user cannot fully predict the long-term negative consequences of using this lethal drug even once.

NICD Classification of Heroin:

Narcotic Analgesic

Scientific name: Diacetyl morphine

Street names: Dope, junk, H, Horse

Medical uses: Though once used as a painkiller, there is no prescribed medical use for heroin in the United States today.

Illicit uses: Users take heroin recreationally to

Methadone and Other Opiate Substitutes

Doctors prescribe methodone to help drug-dependent users manage opiate addiction. It is a synthetic opiate that is taken orally once a day. It suppresses the symptoms of heroin withdrawal for about twenty-four hours. Taking methadone orally, the user does not experience the high associated with heroin, and since it has a long-acting effect, the ups and downs of the heroin dose are eliminated. It comes in several forms. During blind trials, users could not distinguish between the effects of heroin and methadone. Users' main complaint is that a methadone high is not as strong as that produced with heroin. Withdrawal from methadone can take up to a month or longer. According to studies, about two-thirds of addicts who go on methadone will eventually stop using heroin.

Other substitutes for heroin include LAAM, a synthetic opiate, and buprenorphine. Naltrexone helps users stay off heroin after withdrawal. It does not eliminate physical or psychological dependency, but it does block brain receptors so that the user does not achieve the heroin high.

experience its intense high or rush. From then on, a dose is associated with extreme pleasure. Strong drug-seeking behavior commences so the user can repeat the experience.

How obtained: Farmers collect opium poppies and then sell raw opium plant parts to traders. They process it in makeshift labs where the parts are converted into a morphine base. The base is heated and chemicals added. The resulting paste is crushed into powder for sale as heroin. Most of the world's heroin comes from Afghanistan, Pakistan, Mexico, and Colombia, the latter of which is a chief source for drug dealers in the United States.

How taken: Users take heroin primarily as a powder. Pure heroin is white, but the colors range to pink, gray, or brown. Users take powdered heroin in four ways. The powder is dissolved in water and citric acid and injected. When injected, heroin is the fastest-acting of all the opiates and may produce its effects in less than ten seconds. A second method is sniffing or snorting heroin powder through the nose. This eliminates the use of needles and reduces the risk of shared-needle or contaminated-needle infections. Some users try a third method—inhaling the smoke of burning heroin powder that has been heated on metal foil. The fourth way to consume heroin is to swallow the powder, the least common way to take the drug. It is also the most dangerous method because it is almost impossible for the user to know how much can be taken without overdosing. The heroin user may take a dose four times a day.

How heroin works: Once in the bloodstream, heroin reaches the brain where it gets past the brain-blood barrier. This occurs because heroin molecules mimic endorphins, the naturally occurring painkillers that are produced when a body experiences shock or injury. The brain's natural chemistry reacts with heroin toxins to produce a feeling of euphoria or well being. However, an overdose can damage the nervous system and cause harm to the respiratory and cardiovascular systems as well.

Dependency potential: The potential for heroin dependence is the highest of any drug.

Interaction: Mixing heroin with other drugs may intensify the high but increase the risk of the drug itself. Alcohol may be a fatal combination with heroin. Mixing heroin with cocaine into a combination called a Speedball is extremely dangerous to the heart. Heroin, alone or in combination with any substance, can be fatal.

Social dangers: Because heroin is so habit-forming so soon, users may destroy relationships, behavior, health, jobs, and finances in order to obtain the drug.

Legal dangers: It is against the law to sell, buy, or possess heroin in the United States. Possession can mean as much as four years of jail time for a first-time offender. Possession with intent to sell can mean ten to twenty years. About 30 percent of the state prison population in the United States is incarcerated for drug offenses.

Use and withdrawal symptoms: Heroin slows down the body's major processes—respiration, heartbeat, cognitive function, and muscle function. It may cause nausea, confusion, and constipation. It can lead to chemical depression because of changes in the brain caused by the drug. Withdrawal symptoms may be severe—muscle and bone pain, chills and nausea, tremors, cold flashes, vomiting and diarrhea, insomnia, and an intense craving for the drug.

Inhalants

Inhalants are readily available household products that contain a solvent—a chemical in which the product is dissolved. Users inhale the fumes from the solvent to experience effects similar to some illicit drugs. The effect is intoxication similar to alcohol intoxication—slurred speech, a tipsy walk, and uninhibited behavior.

Any substance that gives off a vapor that can be sniffed is an inhalant. Users can find products that produce fumes—nail polish remover, gasoline, cleaning fluids, paint cans, glue—right at home. They are cheap and easy to obtain. For those reasons, inhalants are sometimes the first drug younger teens abuse. Though readily available in grocery and hardware stores, inhalants are not safe for anyone to use in this way. They can and do kill.

Some inhalants make the heart work harder, which may bring on an attack. Some inhaled gases keep oxygen from the lungs. Some users choke on their own vomit. According to some studies, the chronic user can suffer damage to the heart, liver, kidneys, and brain. Toluene, for instance, is one of the main solvents in glue, which is a popular inhalant. Studies show that over a long period, parts of the brain in toluene inhalers actually shrink, causing the user to speak more slowly or to become forgetful. Some inhalants are poisonous, such as benzene, which can drop iron levels in the blood and bring on anemia. Butane, the gas in lighter fuels, can damage the heart.

NICD Classification of Inhalants: *Inhalants*
Scientific name: Manufactured name of many household products
Street names: Same
Medical uses: None
Illicit uses: Users take inhalants recreationally and experimentally to achieve a cheap, fast high.
How obtained: Solvents and aerosol household products are readily available. Some users obtain medical inhalants illegally.
How taken: Users usually sniff inhalants, sometimes covering their heads with a plastic bag for greater, faster effect.
How inhalants work: When a user sniffs inhalants, the fumes go directly to the lungs. The

Computer Dusting Aerosols

In 2005, parents in the United States and Canada learned of an increasing and highly dangerous way for teens to get high, called computer dusting. About 150 deaths from this inhalation practice have been reported among American youths. The teens who died had inhaled the contents of aerosol computer dusting products. The chemicals in these cans produce a mild high for a few minutes. However, in some cases, excessive inhalation resulted in brain damage or death. Such deaths, as with others due to inhalation of toxic fumes, is called Sudden Sniffing Death Syndrome. It can and has occurred on the first try of this dangerous practice.

"Teens inhaling the gases is a scourge of the industry," said an aerosol manufacturer. Apparently, teens who try this believe the lack of volatile substances in computer dusting products makes the practice safe.

"Completely false," says a researcher at the Canadian Centre on Substance Abuse in Ottawa. Aerosol manufacturers are considering adding a substance with a bitter taste in the cans to stop the practice.

inhaled chemicals enter the bloodstream and move to the brain. There they act in a similar manner to anesthetics. They direct the brain to dampen the body's major functions. A person feels floaty, strange, and out of it as respiratory, cardiovascular, speech, and motor centers slow down.

Dependency potential: Some frequent inhalant users become dependent on inhalants and experience withdrawal symptoms.

Social dangers: Inhalants may produce the risky, uninhibited behavior that can occur with alcohol or heroin.

Legal dangers: Sniffing vapors from household products may not be illegal, but the actions that result—fighting or disorderly conduct—may endanger users or get them arrested.

Use and withdrawal symptoms: Inhalant users may suffer the same sort of reaction as alcoholics do when they give up drinking—sweating, shaking, and an extreme urge to take the drug. Headaches and irritability occur. Some heavy users experience hallucinations when they try to withdraw.

Ketamine

Ketamine is a dissociative hallucinogen that is manufactured in laboratories. Like Ecstasy, it is part of the club or rave drug scene. That means it is a drug of choice at dance parties where young people gather to get high. Unlike Ecstasy, however, ketamine produces a kind of dreamy mood—sometimes a sense that the mind is separated from the body and that one is floating in space. Users called this walking into a "K-hole." This dreamy or separated mood can change with higher doses when the user may develop a frightening sense of being disoriented or near death.

NICD Classification of Ketamine:

Hallucinogen

Scientific name: Ketalar and Ketaset are registered trade names

Street names: Bump, Cat valium, Honey oil, K, Special K

Medical uses: Ketamine was developed in the early 1960s as an anesthetic for small animals and also came into use as an anesthetic for human patients undergoing surgery.

Illicit uses: Drug users take ketamine to experience its calming, hallucinatory effects, which enhance certain social experiences, particularly in the club scene.

How taken: Veterinarian and anesthesiologists use liquid ketamine to prepare animals and humans for surgery. Recreational illicit users take ketamine as a powder to snort, or they press it into pill form.

How obtained: Ketamine is legal for veterinary and anesthetic medical use and illegal for any other purpose.

How ketamine works: In medical settings, ketamine is administered as a liquid. Recreational users swallow liquid ketamine or smoke or snort it in powder form. After ketamine enters the bloodstream, it is carried to the brain. The drug affects neurotransmitters in the brain that reduce pain. In ten to twenty minutes, users may feel as though they are floating or unable to move. Ketamine may distort the senses, causing a mild "dreamy" effect. At high doses, users may experience an out-of-body or near-death sensation.

Dependency potential: Illicit users may become habituated to ketamine use in certain social settings—"raves," clubs, and at home with friends.

Interaction: Some researchers say that mixing ketamine with any other drug is highly dangerous.

Social dangers: Ketamine is one of the so-called date rape or rave drugs. Odorless and colorless, it can be slipped into a drink without the victim's awareness. The ensuing numbing sensation compromises a victim's ability to make decisions about safety. After an attack, the victim may not remember the sexual assault.

Legal dangers: Ketamine is an illegal drug except for veterinary or certain medical uses.

Use and withdrawal symptoms: Besides the fact that users may have trouble recalling what happened to them after a dose, ketamine can produce vomiting, nausea, and numbness. It can also result in severe depression and respiratory problems at high doses.

LSD

In the 1960s, it seemed as though every American was familiar with the drug called LSD, or lysergic acid diethylamide. That was in large part due to the so-called psychedelic drug craze of the era when young people known as hippies called for tuning out mainstream society and tuning in the culture to mind-altering drugs. Many mainstream members of society also took LSD. Even into the late 1970s, some LSD users attended such events as light shows where blazing, swirling colors competed with mind-throbbing sounds, all intended to induce a sensory high. The use of LSD declined after that, re-emerged in the 1990s, then dropped back again.

LSD is a synthetic hallucinogen, manufactured in the laboratory. A chemist for Sandoz Laboratories first developed the drug in 1938 while experimenting with compounds he thought might aid those with respiratory problems. This white, colorless substance is one of the most powerful known hallucinogens.

NISD Classification of LSD: *Hallucinogen*
Scientific name: The original name for the drugs known as hallucinogens was Phantastica. In the 1960s, LSD and other such drugs were termed psychedelic by Humphrey Osmond, a British psychiatrist. The name means "mind-manifesting."
Street names: Acid, Blotter acid, Microdots, Sugar Cubes, Trip, Windowpanes, Zen
Medical uses: LSD has no medical uses.

Illicit uses: LSD users take this hallucinogen illegally and recreationally to achieve its effects on perceptions—hallucinations and distortions of reality.

How taken: Crystalline LSD is dissolved in alcohol, put on sugar cubes or blotter paper, and usually swallowed. The drug is so powerful that a small amount can produce intense effects.

How obtained: LSD is illegal in the United States. However, it is produced in various illegal laboratories and distributed through illicit networks of drug dealers.

How LSD works: LSD reaches the brain in about sixty to ninety minutes after the user swallows it. The drug acts on the brain's neurotransmitters to distort the senses and alter perceptions of time and space. The result is a spiritual feeling in some users—the sense that they have found the answers to the problems of the world. Some see bright colors and have a heightened sense of music and motion. More often, reasoning and judgment are seriously impaired. Some users have jumped off buildings and bridges, convinced they were able to fly. Some have vivid nightmares and unpleasant flashbacks, including long lasting personality changes.

Dependency potential: Although LSD does not lead to strong cravings for the drug, a tolerance level does develop. Users become less responsive to the initial dose and begin to take higher doses to get the same initial effect. If LSD is taken for a few days in a row, it will not produce the desired hallucinations regardless of the dose.

Interaction: There is no confirmed interaction with other drugs.

Social dangers: Because LSD consumption may impair judgment and perception, the user may not be able to evaluate unsafe situations.

Legal dangers: Selling and possessing LSD is against the law.

Use and withdrawal symptoms: LSD does not generally produce the cravings users of other psychoactive drugs often experience. Death is very rare from LSD, but an overdose can lead to complications such as respiratory problems. The greatest danger is that LSD may cause unpredictable behavior that affects judgment and safety.

MARIJUANA AND CERTAIN MISUSED PRESCRIPTION DRUGS ARE MORE LIKELY TO BE MADE IN THE UNITED STATES THAN OTHER DRUGS, SUCH AS COCAINE AND HEROIN, WHICH COME MAINLY FROM ASIA.

4 FROM MARIJUANA TO NICOTINE

In several ways, marijuana and nicotine share similar characteristics. Both are made from plant parts, which a user burns in order to inhale the smoke. Both marijuana and cigarettes contain substances that are harmful to the lungs and heart. Both have strong potential for creating dependency. Yet one drug, marijuana, is an illegal drug for everyone in the United States. Cigarettes, on the other hand, are legally available almost anywhere to consumers over eighteen. Why the different legal status?

Tobacco has been part of United States history since the country's founding, when colonists grew tobacco to export to Europe. The prosperity of these early tobacco growers fueled the growth and development of the country. Tobacco growers have long been a political force. They have influenced the government to keep cigarettes available and fought against restrictions on their product. However, several decades ago, consumer health groups began to fight back when the scientific facts about the damaging health consequences of cigarette smoking could no longer be denied. The government, and citizens' health groups, have forced tobacco companies to accept some limitations. Age restrictions on cigarette sales, smoking bans in public places, high tobacco taxes, and public service advertising, paid for by tobacco company lawsuits, have cut the numbers of smokers in half from a century ago.

Marijuana, though once legal, did not share the economic history that tobacco did. Many drug users smoke marijuana, but their numbers are much lower than the numbers of cigarette smokers. Therefore, marijuana profits, though significant, are smaller than from tobacco sales. New research about the damaging effects of marijuana may also have more effect on illicit users than current government restrictions.

Marijuana

Marijuana users generally smoke marijuana and use many methods—complete with drug jargon—in doing so. The most popular forms for smoking marijuana include the cigarettelike joint; the blunt; the bong; the bowl or piece; the shotgun; and the one-hitter. A joint is cigarette-sized. A blunt is a cannabis-cigar made of marijuana and sometimes the wrapper from a regular cigar. A bong is a water pipe that filters cannabis, a method that allows the user to inhale huge amounts in one hit. The bowl or piece is a blown-glass pipe, although some are made from wood or metal. Some homemade pipes use aluminum foil or even soda cans. Glass pipes, called shotguns, have a carburetor that is closed for suction and opened for inhalation. A device that allows the user to inhale small amounts with equal suction is called a one-hitter. Sometimes, the smoker disguises a one-hitter as a real cigarette to cover the fact that he or she is smoking marijuana. Some people eat cannabis raw or mix it with water. With this method, the effects take longer to start but also last longer than smoking. Some experienced smokers take marijuana on an empty stomach to heighten the effects. Cannabis is sometimes also swallowed with grain alcohol, making what is called a Green Dragon, or it is taken as tea.

NICD Classification of Marijuana: *Cannabis*
Scientific name: *Cannabis sativa*
Street names: Boom, Gangster, Grass, Herb, Pot, Mary Jane, Weed—among some two hundred slang terms
How obtained: Although marijuana is illegal in the United States, it is readily available from drug dealers in both large and small cities. Marijuana growers avoid the law by raising their crops in remote areas. Smugglers also bring marijuana into

the United States from Central and South America, Mexico, and other overseas countries.

Medical uses: Debate continues over medical benefits. Some studies cite benefits for treating symptoms of such illnesses as multiple sclerosis, Parkinson's disease, and AIDS. Critics claim more evidence is needed. THC, the active chemical in marijuana, is available in a prescription pill to treat nausea in some cancer and HIV/AIDS patients.

How taken: Users usually smoke marijuana in a cigarette, in a cigar wrapper, or in a pipe. They may sometimes consume it raw or in a marijuana tea.

How marijuana works: Smoked or snorted, marijuana is quickly absorbed through the tissues of the mouth and nose. It reaches a peak effect in about ten minutes if the drug is smoked and in about one hour if marijuana is ingested by mouth. THC (tetrahydrocannabinol), the main ingredient of marijuana, acts on the brain's reward system, which is the part that responds to stimuli such as food and drink. THC stimulates the brain to release the chemical dopa-mine, which sends signals between nerve cells. The signals may transmit feelings of euphoria. Colors and sounds are intensified. When the euphoria passes, the user may become depressed or sleepy. The impaired nerve signals can also produce anxiety, fear, and panic. There is, however, great variance in the content of the smoke. Users report feeling high or floating. Some hours after ingestion, the user may feel the need to sleep for several hours. Upon awakening, the high feeling is gone.

Dependency potential: Long-time, heavy users can become dependent on the drug in much the same way as alcohol abusers do. They, too, develop a habitual craving for the drug and spend unproductive time getting high. Treatment focuses on counseling and group support. There are no medications for treating marijuana dependency at present. One promising therapy, Contingency Management, based on a reward system for marijuana abstinence, has shown some success in retaining marijuana-dependent users in drug treatment programs.

Interaction: Because marijuana is illegal and contains many substances, not many studies of marijuana's interactions with other drugs have produced definitive conclusions.

Social dangers: The use of marijuana can impair a person's ability to drive a car because the drug produces spatial distortions. Drivers' marijuana use has been implicated in many vehicle crashes. Some studies link habitual users of marijuana to lower motivation levels in completing work and achieving goals.

Legal dangers: Marijuana possession is against the law.

Use and withdrawal symptoms: In addition to euphoria, marijuana use can cause short-term memory loss, distorted time perception, and impaired concentration. Physical effects can include dry eyes and mouth, and a rapid heartbeat. Long-term users can develop the kinds of problems seen in heavy smokers. Some animal studies indicate that THC damages cells and tissues that help protect against disease. Other studies suggest a cancer risk from smoking marijuana.

Mescaline

Mescaline is a hallucinogen that occurs naturally in the small, spineless peyote cactus, in the San Pedro cactus, and in the Peruvian Torch cactus. The mescaline molecule is structurally related to adrenaline and noradrenaline, two hormones secreted by the adrenal glands. Both of those compounds have a part in the transmission of nerve impulses.

When European explorers came to the Americas, they discovered that natives of the southwestern United States and northern Mexico had long been using peyote as part of religious ceremonies. But mescaline can also be produced synthetically. It was first identified in 1897 by German scientist Arthur Heffter and became available in 1919. Its side effects can be severe. The drug was made illegal in the United States in 1970 and is prohibited by the 1971 Convention on Psychotropic Substances. CSA classifies it as a Schedule I hallucinogen.

The top of the cactus, called a crown, has disc-shaped buttons that are cut and dried. The buttons may be chewed or soaked in water to produce the intoxicating hallucinogenic effect, which may take two or three hours to begin and may last up to twelve hours. The user may experience a severely altered state of consciousness and visual hallucinations as well as a condition called hallucinogen persisting perception disorder (HPPD).

NICD Classification of Mescaline:
Hallucinogen

Scientific name: 3,4,5-trimethoxyphenethylamine

Street names: Buttons, Cactus, Mesc, Peyote

How obtained: Mescaline is an illegal drug, but it is grown and distributed in the Americas.

Medical uses: None

Illicit uses: Mescaline users take it illegally and recreationally for its hallucinogenic, perception-altering effects.

How taken: Mescaline is either chewed or dissolved in liquid.

How mescaline works: Swallowed as a liquid or chewed, mescaline is absorbed through the bloodstream into the brain. There it acts on neurotransmitters that regulate auditory and visual sensations. The results are heightened emotions and senses as well as impaired judgment and possible panic and anxiety.

Dependency potential: The drug does not have the dependency potential of other psychoactive drugs, such as cocaine, marijuana, or heroin.

Interaction: As with any hallucinogen, mixing mescaline with other drugs can increase the mind-altering experience and intensify physical problems, such as fast heart rate, anxiety, dizziness, and vomiting.

Social dangers: Someone high on mescaline may not have complete control of his or her emotions and judgment.

Legal dangers: Mescaline use is illegal as it is a Schedule I drug in the United States.

Use and withdrawal symptoms: With each dose, the user may or may not experience any one of a number of reactions: distorted visualizations; a feeling of imminent death; a fear of not being able to return to normal consciousness.

Methamphetamine

Methamphetamine, which is derived from amphetamine, strongly affects certain brain systems by blocking the recycling of dopamine. Although chemically related to amphetamines, methamphetamine has a more potent effect on the central nervous system. It is a white, odorless, bitter-tasting powder that dissolves easily in water or alcohol. Its effects last much longer than those of cocaine. According to some reports, it is second in use to marijuana among high school seniors. A National Survey on Drug Use and Health (NSDUH) in 2005 reported that more than 4 percent of Americans had tried methamphetamine at least once. According to the National Institute on Drug Abuse, methamphetamine use was on the increase early in the twenty-first century. For instance, a reported 59 percent of treatments for drug abuse in Hawaii in 2004 concerned methamphetamine. Meth usage in Atlanta, Georgia, jumped from 6.7 percent of treatment admissions in 2002 to 11 percent in the first half of 2004.

One reason for methamphetamine's popularity may be that it is easy to make and obtain. A few hundred dollars in initial expenses result in about a thousand dollars' worth of the potent drug. Meth's affordability and availability make it popular with some drug-taking teens and young adults. Using over-the-counter ingredients, illicit drug makers produce methamphetamine in out-of-the-way laboratories and basements. Battery acid, lantern fuel, lye, hydrochloric acid, and antifreeze are some of the ingredients in methamphetamine.

NICD Classification of Methamphetamine:
Stimulant
Scientific names: methamphetamine
Street names: Crank, Chalk, Crystal, Glass, Ice, Meth, Speed, Road Dope, Tina, Uppers, among others
How obtained: Drug makers produce meth in home labs. Users purchase it from dealers who obtain it from illegal methamphetamine labs.
Medical uses: Limited, primarily in the treatment of obesity.
Illicit use: Users almost instantly desire to repeat the intense high they experience on methamphetamine. Therefore drug-seeking behavior often commences immediately.

How taken: Users take it by mouth; snort the powder; inject; or smoke it.

How methamphetamine works: Methamphetamine enters the bloodstream and works quickly on the brain and central nervous system to block the recycling of the chemical dopamine, which sends signals between nerve cells. This causes pleasure-inducing dopamine to build up. The accumulation of dopamine gives the user a pleasurable rush or flash. If the drug is taken orally, the high can last half a day.

A CHEAP, CONCENTRATED FORM OF METHAMPHETAMINE CALLED "ICE" IS SO WIDELY AVAILABLE BECAUSE DRUG USERS CAN MAKE IT AT HOME. METHAMPHETAMINE USAGE HAS BEEN RAVAGING RURAL COMMUNITIES AND STRETCHING LAW ENFORCEMENT STAFFS ACROSS THE COUNTRY.

Dependency potential: With excessive meth use, a tolerance develops. Users then try to take higher, more frequent doses of the drug to achieve the initial high. In addition to developing dependency, the meth user may exhibit violent behavior, sleeplessness, and mental confusion. Sometimes psychotic disturbances occur, such as the feeling that bugs are crawling on one's skin. This is called formication.

Interaction: Studies show behavioral changes in rats when the drug is used with antihistamines.

Social dangers: Violent behavior is a possible result of overuse. The high is so intense, it impairs normal, responsible behavior and clouds a user's judgment about sexual behaviors. Some bingeing parents on meth forget to watch over their small children, who sometimes witness heavy drug taking at early ages and may suffer from neglect.

Legal dangers: Methamphetamine is illegal in all states.

Use and withdrawal symptoms: While taking the drug, the user may experience heightened alertness and euphoria. At high levels of consumption, the user may become agitated, paranoid, anxious, and aggressive. Physical effects at high doses may increase heartbeat and bring on convulsions, coma, and death. During withdrawal, effects may include depression, excessive fatigue, and irritability. An intense craving for a dose also characterizes use and withdrawal stages.

Methaqualone

A researcher in India discovered methaqualone in the 1950s while conducting a research program for antimalaria drugs. In 1965, a pharmaceutical company introduced methaqualone (trade name Quaalude) as a safe substitute for barbiturates, and it soon became a highly popular sedative. The name Quaalude comes from the phrase "quiet interlude." By 1972, it was considered fashionable on college campuses to "lude out," meaning to take methaqualone with wine. In 1984, the U.S. government placed methaqualone in the CSA's highest classification, Schedule I. Its potential for addiction and the severity of withdrawal symptoms were found to be on a par with barbiturates.

Methaqualone is a sedating, general central nervous system depressant. It was used medically in the 1960s and 1970s as a sleeping pill to treat insomnia and as a sedative. Methaqualone has been withdrawn from the markets of many developed countries because of its dangers of use and potential for abuse.

NICD Classification of Methaqualone:

Depressant

Scientific name: Sold under the trade names of Quaalude, Sopor, and Parest

Street names: Ludes, Sopors

Medical uses: There is no current medical use for the drug in the United States.

Illicit use: Methaqualone users take it recreationally and illegally to achieve a relaxing, euphoric high.

How obtained: Users obtain methaqualone illegally from drug dealers in the United States. It is a Schedule I drug.

How taken: Methaqualone users take it orally in pill or tablet form.

How methaqualone works: In pill or tablet form, methaqualone is swallowed and enters the bloodstream. As with all depressants, when methaqualone reaches the brain, it stimulates the neurotransmitter GABA, which reduces signals between the brain and the central nervous system. With fewer signals from the brain, the lungs, heart, muscle, speech, and cognitive centers all slow down.

Interaction: Mixing the drug with other depressants, especially alcohol, can have severe consequences because the additional depressant enhances GABA activation. That means GABA causes the brain to send fewer signals to the rest of the body. Because both alcohol and methaqualone depress respiration and heart pumping, basic functions that keep the body alive may dangerously slow down or stop entirely.

Social dangers: As with any of the drugs that bring on extreme relaxation, a user may not be able to control actions or reactions in dangerous situations.

Legal dangers: The drug is illegal in the United States.

Use and withdrawal symptoms: Users taking methaqualone may exhibit symptoms similar to alcohol intoxication: slowed reaction time, slurred speech, disorientation. The drug can lower the heart rate and slow breathing to dangerous levels, leading to convulsions, delirium, coma, and death due to cardiac or respiratory arrest.

Morphine

Morphine is the chief active ingredient in opium. It is a powerful analgesic drug that acts directly on the central nervous system to relieve pain. Morphine is highly addictive. Both physical and psychological dependence quickly develop.

In the early 1800s, Friedrich Serturner, a German pharmacist, was looking for the perfect pain reliever. He became the first to isolate what he called *morphia* from opium. It was named for Morpheus, the Greek god of dreams. In 1831 Serturner was awarded the Nobel Prize. The use of morphine spread quickly after the development of the hypodermic needle in 1853. The drug's chief uses were pain relief and as a possible cure for opium addiction. Morphine was administered both orally and by injection during the U.S. Civil War to ease the pain of injuries and emergency surgery on the battlefield. Some reports say that morphine dependence was heavy among the soldiers.

People continued to use morphine through the nineteenth century. Drug takers were seemingly unaware of its dangers or its potential for dependency that could endanger the users' health, personal lives, and work. Doctors prescribed the drug for the pain of childbirth and for anxiety and fatigue. The idea that it was better to replace a bad habit with one less evil led to the use of morphine for alcohol addiction. The drug was said to reduce violent behavior in alcoholics. Whereas it might be unseemly for a lady to drink alcohol in some circles, a small libation laced with morphine to reduce anxiety was considered almost fashionable. After heroin was derived from morphine in 1874, morphine use fell. However, even today, if the supply of heroin becomes scarce, users seek morphine as a substitute.

NICD Classification of Morphine: *Narcotic*
Scientific name: *Papaver somniferum*
Street names: Dreamer, Miss Emma, Morf
How obtained: Medical morphine is legally manufactured from parts of opium plants grown in Tasmania and other countries. Illicit users sometimes obtain it from illegal use of prescriptions.
Medical uses: Morphine is legally used in hospitals for surgery pain; in the relief of severe chronic pain; and for certain conditions such as diarrhea associated with AIDS.
Illicit uses: Illegally, morphine is used as a substitute for heroin or other illicit drugs that produce a more intense high.

Better Than Morphine?

Under controlled use, morphine is one of the world's most effective painkillers. Whether taken by mouth or by injection, morphine reduces the severe pain from cancer, kidney stones, or physical injury. It relieves anxiety before surgery. It may reduce the amount of anesthetic needed during surgery. But is morphine on the way out? In November 2006, researchers in France said they have found a natural painkiller that is "six times more powerful than morphine," without its addictive and psychological side effects. Called opiorphin, it comes from human saliva. Researchers warn that although it seems to be as effective as morphine, opiorphin must still be tested for possible side effects.

How taken: Orally as a concentrated solution, powder, or tablet form. By injection, morphine produces an intense sensation in the muscles, delivering a powerful "rush" and relief from pain.

How morphine works: As all opiates do, morphine mimics endorphins, the painkillers that occur naturally in the human body. Morphine travels quickly throughout the central nervous system, prohibiting pain signals from reaching the brain even though the original source of the pain remains.

Dependency potential: Morphine is highly likely to lead to craving and dependence.

Interaction: The most serious interactions are with other drugs that have sedation effects.

Social dangers: Craving for the drug causes habitual morphine users to compromise relationships, work, and finances in order to obtain the drug. Moreover, morphine's sedative effects—along with the dependency potential—make it difficult for a user to function well in everyday life.

Legal dangers: Prescribed morphine is legal. Otherwise it is not.

Use and withdrawal symptoms: Morphine relieves pain. It also produces euphoria, lethargy, drowsiness, blurred vision, and constipation. It can lead to dependence as well as respiratory distress. In high doses, morphine may be fatal. Withdrawal symptoms can include restlessness, heavy perspiration, gooselike flesh, eye tearing, and restless sleep.

Nicotine

For use and abuse, it is hard to beat the nicotine in tobacco. Despite the endless studies over the past few decades that point to nicotine as a cause of lung cancer and other respiratory diseases, despite the studies that show even secondhand smoke to be dangerous to one's health, despite the federal and state laws banning tobacco in public areas, despite all the facts that cannot be denied about tobacco's bodily harm, people still smoke.

There are no medicinal benefits to smoking tobacco. Its use is one of the most preventable causes of illness or death in the United States. It leads to clear physical dependence, and it has been proven to be extremely harmful over most smokers' lifetimes. So, why do people continue to use it?

The reason is nicotine. It is a powerful psycho-stimulant contained in tobacco. In any form, it is absorbed in varying amounts into the user's bloodstream. In a short time, tolerance and dependence often follow. (A small subgroup of smokers, called *chippers,* smoke but do not always develop dependence.) Most users get hooked quickly. Smokers continue their habit because they just can't stop. Nicotine abuse is one of the most difficult of all addictions to overcome.

Tobacco has a long history in America. John Rolfe is said to have been the first to raise tobacco for commercial use at the Jamestown, Virginia settlement in 1612. It was a thriving tobacco-based community by the time of his death in 1622. The colony of Virginia, as well as the Carolinas, were prosperous tobacco producers during the seventeenth and eighteenth centuries. About a third of the internal revenue tax collected by the U.S. government until about the 1880s came from the tobacco excise tax.

According to historians, just about everybody smoked or chewed tobacco in the late 1800s in America. Wrote Ellis Oberholtzer in his *A History of the United States since the Civil War:* "The chewing of tobacco was well-nigh universal. . . . Homes and public buildings were supplied with spittoons. Even the pews of fashionable churches were likely to contain these familiar conveniences. . . . An observant traveller in the South . . . said that in his belief that seven-tenths of all persons above the age of twelve years, both male and female, used tobacco in some form. . . . Boys of eight or nine years of age and half-grown girls smoked."

In the twentieth century, smoking was seen as glamorous and sophisticated, portrayed in hundreds of movies and later on the television screen. Teenagers couldn't wait to be "grown-up enough" to take a cigarette, if they hadn't already done so. It was not until mid-century that health concerns over smoking began to be raised to the general public. Even when health warnings were posted on cigarette packages and in ads, no one paid too much attention and the tobacco companies loudly defended their product.

99

Tobacco and the Changing Laws: What's Next?

1933 Agricultural Adjustment Act is passed to aid tobacco farmers as the market dropped.

1935 Tobacco Inspection Act develops tobacco grade standards.

1938 Agricultural Adjustment Act is passed again to authorize market quotas.

1949 Agricultural Act passed again, this time to authorize price supports.

1950 Morton Levin publishes an article in *JAMA* (*Journal of the American Medical Association*) claiming smoking is linked to lung cancer.

1954 The Tobacco Industry Research Committee takes out a nationwide, two-page ad saying any studies that link smoking and lung cancer are inconclusive.

1964 First Surgeon General's report is released saying cigarette smoking is causally related to lung cancer in men.

1966 Federal Cigarette Labeling and Advertising Act requires health warnings but only on cigarette packages.

1969 Public Health Cigarette Smoking Act carries the following warning: The Surgeon General Has Determined That Cigarette Smoking Is Dangerous to Your Health.

1971 Cigarette ads are banned on television.

1973 Little Cigar Act bans TV and radio advertising of little cigars.

1977 First Great American Smokeout. Film called *Death in the West* with smoking cowboys dying of lung disease is shown throughout the country.

1980 Surgeon General notes the rise of lung cancer death rates in women.

1984 Warning labels must appear in a special format on cigarette packages and most advertising.

1986 Comprehensive Smokeless Tobacco Health Education Act extends broadcast advertising ban to smokeless tobacco items.

1994 Seven tobacco companies testify in congressional hearings. Their executives say nicotine is not addictive.

1995 Two studies indicate an increase in smoking among minors. California bans smoking in restaurants.

1997 President Clinton signs an order making all government workplaces smoke free.

1998 Phillip Morris tobacco company announces that there is "no safe cigarette."

1999–2006 Delaware, New York, Connecticut, Maine, Massachusetts, New Jersey, Rhode Island, Vermont, and Washington all pass laws banning smoking in bars and restaurants.

2006–2007 Ohio, Nevada, and Arizona ban smoking in most public places.

Today, cigarettes and other tobacco products, as well as most ads for alcohol, are nearly banned from all television networks.

CIGARETTE SMOKING CAUSES MAJOR HEALTH PROBLEMS, YET CIGARETTES ARE LESS REGULATED THAN OTHER DRUGS THAT ALSO CAUSE WIDESPREAD HEALTH PROBLEMS.

Eventually, even the tobacco companies could not ignore the link between smoking and lung cancer and other diseases.

According to *World Almanac* statistics, cigarette smoking in general has been on the decrease since about 1975, including among eighth, tenth, and twelfth graders. More than 30 percent of those in the tenth and twelfth grades claim to have tried cigarettes, and fewer than 50 percent of eighth graders say they have smoked.

What are the effects of cigarette smoking? According to the Tobacco Information and Prevention Source (TIPS), smoking:

- results in lower lung function than among nonsmokers.

- causes stroke and heart disease; teens who smoke show early signs of these diseases.
- increases the resting heart rate of young adults.
- increases the risk of lung cancer.
- is associated with emotional or psychological ailments.
- is damaging to physical fitness in teens in terms of performance and endurance.
- is associated with alcohol use.
- shortens life span by thirteen to fourteen years for smokers compared with nonsmokers.

Because the nicotine in tobacco smoke is a stimulant, smoking can energize, reduce stress, and relieve boredom. The effects are immediate, which is why it is easy to become addicted to tobacco.

Classification of Nicotine: *Stimulant*
Scientific name: *Nicotiana tabacum*
Street names: Chewing tobacco, Cigarettes, Cigars, Snuff, Weeds
How obtained: Adults in the United States over eighteen can legally purchase cigarettes and other tobacco products.
Medical uses: None
Illicit uses: Because cigarettes are widely available legally, underage teens find it fairly easy to obtain cigarettes and begin a smoking habit.

How taken: Smokers inhale nicotine in the smoke of cigarettes, cigars, and pipe tobacco. Or they may swallow nicotine when they chew tobacco or nicotine gum during the first period of trying to give up cigarettes.

How nicotine works: When someone smokes, inhales, or chews tobacco products, the chemical nicotine is released. It is absorbed by the lungs and moves into the bloodstream, then reaches the brain in less than eight seconds. Nicotine activates the brain receptors involved in body functions such as breathing, heart rate, memory, and muscle movement. It also releases the chemical dopamine, which transmits feelings of reward and pleasure. Nicotine is quickly metabolized and leaves the body in a few hours, which creates the need for greater and more frequent use.

Nicotine has damaging effects on the cardiovascular system, such as lowering good cholesterol even in young smokers. It can cause heart muscles to lose elasticity, raising the risk of stroke. Smoking is a leading cause of lung cancer and is involved in respiratory diseases such as emphysema. It restricts blood vessels, which can lead to bad skin and often causes halitosis, or persistent bad breath. Smoking may limit a person's daily physical activities due to decreased circulation and shortness of breath.

Dependency potential: Nicotine has high potential for causing dependence.

Interaction: Many smokers also use alcohol regularly. Some mouth, neck, and throat cancers are associated with the use of these two drugs in combination over a long period of time.

Social dangers: Nicotine, in the form of cigarettes, is often the first drug a teen tries. Once that first use barrier has been crossed, teen smokers may find it easier to move on to other damaging drugs, such as alcohol and marijuana. This is the reason nicotine is sometimes described as a "gateway drug." Nonetheless, whether or not a new smoker moves on to other drugs, nicotine causes many damaging effects all by itself—dependency and many kinds of physical harm in those who are unable to give up the habit.

Legal dangers: Buying tobacco products is legal for adults.

Use and withdrawal symptoms: In many smokers, persistent and prolonged use of tobacco products will result in irreparable physical damage that cannot be repaired if nicotine abuse goes on for too many years. However, if a new smoker quits after a short period of use, respiratory problems and other risks will gradually improve. The Food and Drug Administration has approved several medications to help the smoker quit the habit: Bupropion, nicotine inhaler, and nicotine nasal spray. These are all available by prescription. Nicotine gum is available over-the-counter, and the nicotine patch is available by prescription and over-the-counter. These nicotine products are transitional aids to help users kick the nicotine habit for good.

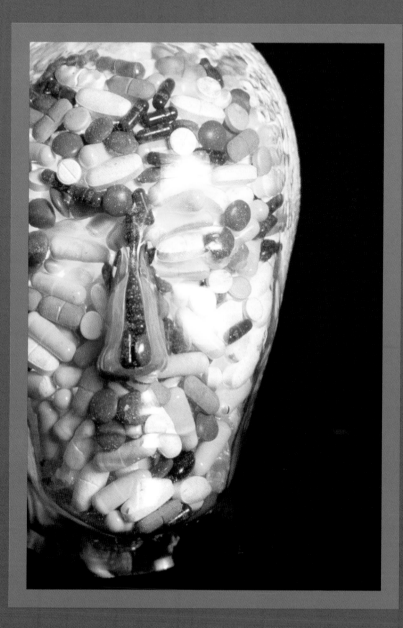

THE MOLECULES OF PSYCHOACTIVE DRUGS GAIN ACCESS TO THE BRAIN BY MIMICKING BRAIN CHEMICALS CALLED NEUROTRANSMITTERS. ONCE INSIDE THE BRAIN, THE DRUG MOLECULES AFFECT LEVELS OF THESE NEUROTRANSMITTERS AS WELL AS THE SPEED AT WHICH THE BRAIN RELEASES THEM.

5 FROM OPIATES TO ROHYPNOL

The camera closes in on a father driving his son to a game. The dialogue begins with the dad casually asking the son about his friends' interest in taking drugs. The public-service ad ends with the statement: "Parents, the Anti-drug." Is this true? Are involved, caring parents the anti-drug that stands between their children and drug experimentation, usage, and eventual dependence? The answer is yes. Teens who spend daily face time with parents who are neither too strict nor too lax, who show pride in them, and in whom the teens feel they can confide, experiment and use drugs much less than teens whose parents do not exhibit those parenting styles. Teens from supportive families say the main reason they experiment less with smoking, drinking, or misusing prescription drugs, no matter what the drug scene at school, is that they don't want to let down their parents. So parents can be more powerful than opiates, opioids such as Oxycontin, or PCP—all with the potential of creating dependence in users young and old.

Opiates

Opium, and drugs made from it, have been used and abused for centuries. It may well be the first discovered drug. Ancient Egyptians used opium. The Sumerians, who lived in what is now Iraq, used it in 3400 BCE. Ancient Greeks found that it calmed fears and anxiety. The Romans knew it as a painkiller and a people killer as well. They used opium in both suicides and assassinations. By the seventeenth century, the Turks had found a new way to use opium. Instead of chewing the leaves or drinking tea made from them, they began to heat the leaves and smoke them. People became so dependent on the drug that Turkish doctors declared it to be dangerous, and its use declined there. In other parts of the world, including China and the United States, opium was often regarded as a cure for toothache pain and anxiety in the 1800s. Opium-based medicines treated gout and cholera, among other maladies.

Opium became popular in the United States after the California gold rush of 1849 to 1860. Many Chinese people immigrated to America during that time, bringing with them the custom of opium dens. These were quiet rooms where customers could buy and use opium in peace and security. At first it was said that the only users were the Chinese, but historians report that some cowboys of the Old West were opium users as well. Today, both legal and illegal cultivation of opium occurs chiefly in Asia. Its legal uses are for producing morphine and codeine used in many places around the world to treat pain and coughing.

NICD Classification of Opiates: *Narcotic*
Scientific name: *Papaver somniferum*
Street names: Joy Plant, Skee, Poppy, Auntie, Zero
How obtained: Opium's pharmaceutical use is strictly controlled. Opium users obtain the drug and other drugs made from it from drug dealers.
Medical uses: Derivatives of opium, such as morphine and codeine, are used to control pain and coughing.
Illicit uses: The opiate of choice today is likely to be heroin, but if a user cannot get it, he or she will sometimes substitute opium derivatives—morphine or codeine. These produce similar, though less intense, effects than heroin.
How taken: Medically, users administer opium derivatives by injection or drink it in codeine-added syrups. Illicit opium is smoked or injected.
How opiates work: Smoked, injected, or swallowed as a liquid medication, opium—or its derivatives morphine and codeine—quickly travel through the bloodstream to the brain. Acting much like

109

endorphins, the body's naturally occurring painkillers, opium blocks the pain receptors in various parts of the body. They cannot send pain signals back to the brain. So the user experiences relief even through the original source of the pain remains. At higher doses, users of opium and opium-based drugs experience a feeling of contentment.

Dependency potential: As with all opiates, opium use rapidly leads to dependence.

Interaction: Opium's effects are more dangerous and intense when combined with other drugs. Because opium has a sedating effect, when it is combined with other sedating drugs or depressants, it may lower respiration and heart rate to dangerously low levels.

Social dangers: Users of opium and its derivatives, morphine and codeine, may engage in drug-seeking behavior at the expense of personal relationships, jobs, and financial security.

Legal dangers: Opium is an illegal substance except when prescribed for certain medical conditions.

Use and withdrawal symptoms: Opiate use produces both euphoria and drowsiness. It can cause vomiting, diarrhea, and respiratory distress. Regular use may lead to tolerance and dependence, especially if the drug is taken to induce euphoria rather than for pain relief.

Opioids

Opioids, such as OxyContin, Percocet, and Percodan, are legally prescribed pain relievers. They are synthetic drugs, meaning they are artificially produced, not cultivated as are opium poppies. Opioids produce similar effects to naturally grown opium and its derivatives, though in prescribed doses the effects are not as intense.

Some illegal drug users and dealers have discovered that crushing an Oxycontin pill and snorting or sniffing it produces a feeling of euphoria. This has resulted in illegal trade. Some people who have legal access to the pills sell them at a huge profit. Some manage to get multiple prescriptions for the drug from doctors who do not ask too many questions. Since 2001, there have been reports of numerous deaths from opioid overdose. An article in *USA Today*, November 2006, reported an increased use of Oxycontin by teens.

NICD Classification of Opioids: *Narcotic*
Scientific names: Oxycodone, which includes OxyContin, Percocet, Percodan, and others
Street names: Hillbilly Heroin, Oxycotton, Kicker
Medical uses: Powerful pain reliever
Illicit uses: Users take illegally obtained Oxycodone drugs recreationally, as a fairly available substitute for heroin or morphine, or because they have become dependent on the drugs for a condition they may have had or still have.

How obtained: Oxycodone prescriptions are legal for medical uses. However, there is a thriving black market for these drugs.

How taken: As prescribed, Oxycodone pills are swallowed. Used illegally, the drugs are crushed and either chewed or snorted. The crushed pill can also be mixed with water and injected into a vein.

How Oxycodone drugs work: Oxycodone drugs, when swallowed or injected, attach to opioid receptors. These are natural proteins in the brain, spinal cord, and gastrointestinal tract. Once attached, Oxycodone molecules are able to block the pain signals that the brain sends to various parts of the body. In addition to blocking pain, Oxycodone drugs create euphoric feelings and provide relief from anxious feelings.

The legally prescribed tablet has a slow-release coating that supplies pain relief for up to twelve hours. But when the tablet is crushed—which illegal users do—the slow-release coating disappears and the sniffed powder reacts much like heroin—delivering a quick, powerful rush that easily leads to dependence.

Dependency potential: Used illegally, Oxycodone drugs readily lead to dependence.

Social dangers: Hundreds of deaths occur each year from the overdose or interaction of Oxycodone drugs alone or with other drugs when high overdose levels depress critical processes in the body.

Pharm Parties: The New High?

A new trend is the "pharm party"—teenagers getting together to experiment with all types of prescription drugs. Taking drugs from the family medicine cabinet is called "pharming," and bowls of prescription drugs mixed together are known as trail mix.

However the drugs are obtained, the partygoers each bring a prescription drug to share. They frequently combine their drugs with alcohol or marijuana.

Because the United States Food and Drug Administration approves all legal prescription drugs, experts say that in the minds of many teens, the FDA approval makes these drugs legal to consume. However, they are only legal for the person who owns the prescription. They are not necessarily safe for anyone else, and certainly not safe when mixed with other drugs. The most common examples of prescription drugs at pharm parties are: painkilling opioids, such as Vicodin and OxyContin; depressants that treat panic or sleep disorders, such as Valium and Xanax; and drugs for hyperactivity, such as Ritalin.

Legal dangers: Because they are so readily available in legal prescription form, Oxycodone use is difficult to control. However, these drugs, when unprescribed or misused as prescribed, are illegal.

Use and withdrawal symptoms: Oxycodone drug use may cause depression of respiratory function, nausea, coma, and possible death. Withdrawing from Oxycodone drug use can bring on several days of flulike symptoms, including nausea, dizziness, diarrhea, vomiting, and tremors. In some cases, withdrawal symptoms are so severe that users must undergo detoxification programs in a hospital. The deaths that occur with an overdose are mainly due to a lack of oxygen, which leads to respiratory failure.

PCP

Phencyclidine, or PCP, is a drug with potentially devastating hallucinogenic effects on users. Its effects are similar to those of LSD but can be much more dangerous. Known for producing severe physical reactions, such as coma, there is no way to predict who will experience dangerous effects from taking PCP. Although it is classified as a hallucinogen, PCP also acts as a depressant, stimulant, and anesthetic and can induce unpredictable reactions in users.

PCP was first tested as an anesthesia for surgery after World War I, but research was stopped because the side effects were too severe. The

114

Parke-Davis pharmaceutical company developed phencyclidine as an anesthetic with the name of Sernyl in the 1950s. Patients quite often became irrational while recovering from it. Later, it was marketed as an anesthesia for veterinary surgery, named Sernylan, but was once again discontinued because of severe side effects. It is a Schedule II drug in the United States. In its 2004 annual survey of Americans age twelve and older, the Substance Abuse and Mental Health Services Administration reported that lifetime use of PCP was on the decline for those eighteen to twenty-five, but that use by twelve- and thirteen-year-olds was increasing, though the numbers remain small.

In its original state, PCP is a white, crystalline powder that is readily soluble, although its bitter taste is distinctive. The psychoactive effects may last only hours, but PCP may not be totally eliminated from the body for weeks. It is called a dissociative drug because it distorts sight and sound perceptions and gives the user a feeling of being detached from him or herself and the rest of the world.

NICD Classification of PCP: *Hallucinogen*
Scientific name: *phenylcyclohexyl pyrrolidine*
Street names: PCP, Angel Dust, Ozone, Rocket Fuel, Supergrass, Wack. When used with marijuana, it is called Crystal Supergrass and Killer Joints. When taken with Ecstasy, the practice is called Elephant Flipping.

115

Medical uses: PCP is now an illegal drug, occasionally used by veterinarians.

Illicit uses: PCP is an illicit recreational drug that users take to alter their perceptions.

How obtained: Although illegal, PCP is a synthetic chemical produced in illicit labs for recreational use in a number of large North American cities.

How taken: Most commonly sold as a powder or liquid, PCP is smoked, snorted, injected, or ingested. It is also available as a tablet or capsule. When it is smoked, which is called "getting wet," it is usually first applied to a leafy material such as parsley or marijuana. The liquid into which the cigarette is dipped is often called "embalming fluid."

How PCP works: Whether smoked, swallowed, or injected, PCP travels through the bloodstream and reaches the brain, where it acts to depress neurotransmitters. The result is often confusion and disorientation shortly after the dose—within a few minutes if inhaled or injected, or a half hour if taken by mouth. Blood pressure and heart rate increase, and tremors are common.

Dependency potential: PCP use can lead to craving and compulsive and aggressive behavior as the dependent user seeks the drug.

Interaction: Sometimes used with marijuana or Ecstasy. Any combination with this drug is a danger. Its use with alcohol and other depressants may result in coma because PCP enhances depressive effects.

Social dangers: During the disorientation and uncoordinated effects that are part of a PCP high, the user is usually incapable of driving a car safely. PCP also impairs judgment of unsafe situations, putting the user at risk. Such PCP effects can impair the user for as long as a day.

Legal dangers: PCP is an illegal Schedule II drug in the United States.

Use and withdrawal symptoms: When some PCP users are brought to emergency rooms with an overdose, they may be suicidal or violent. Nonetheless, no scientific evidence definitively proves that PCP induces violence. Low to moderate usage may produce shallow breathing, elevated blood pressure and pulse rate, profuse sweating, and a general numbness of the arms and legs. At high doses, blood pressure and pulse rate drop, and breathing slows. Loss of balance, blurred vision, and dizziness may occur. Speech may be garbled. Hallucinations and delusions are noted. Coma and death may result, although some deaths are due to accident or suicide. Long-term PCP use may lead to speech difficulties, memory loss, and depression lasting as long as a year.

Psilocybin

Psilocybin is a hallucinogen and a naturally occurring compound that comes from different types of mushrooms found in the southern United States and parts of Mexico and South America. The mushrooms contain up to .04 percent of psilocybin, and they are added to other food because of their bitter flavor or brewed as tea. Psilocybin can also be produced synthetically, although there is not much evidence of such usage. Effects of this drug may be compared to, but do not last as long as, LSD.

Psilocybin mushrooms have been used for hundreds of years. Native people believe psilocybin use enables them to contact the spirit world. Recreational drug use began to take hold in the 1960s in the United States.

NICD Classification of Psilocybin:
Hallucinogen

Scientific name: Psilocybin is found in many species of fungi, including the genus *Psilocybe*

Street names: Boomers, Magic Mushrooms, Shrooms, Silly Putty; when used with Ecstasy, Flower flipping or Hippieflip.

How obtained: The drug is often available illegally from drug dealers and from the Internet. Users may also illegally purchase kits to cultivate the mushrooms at home.

Medical uses: A study supported by Multidisciplinary Association for Psychedelic Studies (MAPS) began in 2001 to look into psilocybin effects on patients with obsessive-compulsive disorder. There is also some interest in studying its effects on cluster headaches.

Illicit uses: Today, the drug is popular at so-called rave parties and on college campuses.

NATIVE PEOPLE IN THE NORTHERN AND SOUTHERN AMERICAN HEMISPHERES LONG USED EXTRACTS OF THE PSILOCYBE MUSHROOM DURING CEREMONIES AND RITUALS. IN THE MID–1900S, DRUG USERS LEARNED OF THIS MUSHROOM'S POTENTIAL FOR ALTERING PERCEPTIONS, AND AN ILLICIT TRADE IN THE MUSHROOMS BEGAN.

According to the University of Michigan's Monitoring the Future Survey, a little more than 9 percent of high school seniors used hallucinogens other than LSD, a category that includes psilocybin, at least once.

How taken: Usually eaten raw, whether fresh or dried. The mushrooms have long slender stems with caps. If boiled in water, the water is swallowed. The drug may also be stewed or mixed in a soup or salad. A few users inject mushroom juice.

How psilocybin works: As with all hallucinogens, psilocybin (whether eaten fresh or dried) enters the bloodstream and stimulates the brain by acting on neurotransmitters that affect sensory perceptions. Feelings of elation or sadness may intensify. All sensory perceptions may heighten and become distorted. The user can also develop extreme anxiety or panic after a dose, and a so-called bad trip can last for hours.

Dependency potential: The drug does not usually produce cravings in most users, yet some do develop an ongoing desire to repeat the hallucinogenic experience.

Social dangers: Because drowsiness and a lack of coordination may develop, the user may not be able to judge unsafe situations or drive a car.

Legal dangers: It is illegal to possess and sell psilocybin mushrooms.

Use and withdrawal symptoms: When the dose takes effect, common reactions are impaired judgment, mental and physical relaxation, a sense of being separated from surroundings, distortions, and mood swings. Sweating, nausea, anxiety, and numbness may all indicate the onset of overdose. The effects of this drug are unpredictable, depending on the amount, the user's mood, and the atmosphere in which the drug taking occurs. A bad trip, as with LSD, is common. Flashbacks, in which a user experiences the effects of the drug without taking it again, may occur.

Ritalin

Ritalin is the trade name for methylphenidate, legally prescribed for children who suffer from attention deficit hyperactivity disorder (ADHD). Children with these behavior problems typically have short attention spans or cannot follow instructions. They may fidget excessively. Ritalin has a calming effect on children with ADHD. However, illicit users who do not have ADHD experience Ritalin's stimulatory effects.

NICD Classification of Ritalin: *Stimulant*
Scientific name: Methylphenidate
Street names: Chill pill, Kiddie cocaine
How obtained: Legally by prescription. Users without a prescription sometimes obtain the drug illicitly from others who do have a prescription.
Medical uses: Ritalin calms anxiety, especially in children.
Illicit uses: Ritalin has become popular among high school and college students as an illicit drug that makes them feel more alert.

How taken: Doctors prescribe Ritalin in pill form. Illicit users sometimes crush the pills into a powder that they snort or mix in water and inject with a syringe.

How Ritalin works: When swallowed and absorbed, Ritalin becomes a stimulant on the central nervous system, yet produces a calming effect in hyperactive children. The drug seems to increase the release of the chemical dopamine, which sends signals between nerve cells in the body.

Dependency potential: Illicit Ritalin abusers may depend on the drug when they want to experience its stimulatory effects. However, it does not usually lead to serious dependency problems.

Interaction: Adverse reactions are associated with combining Ritalin with other substances.

Social dangers: Illicit users may depend on the drug to feel alert instead of making positive lifestyle changes to function with more alertness.

Legal dangers: Ritalin is a legal drug by prescription only. Those who sell Ritalin illegally risk felony charges.

Use and withdrawal symptoms: By increasing certain brain neurotransmitters, Ritalin also increases heart rate and blood pressure. Skin rash, stomach pains, digestive problems, weight loss, nausea, and vomiting may occur. Its use may damage the nose tissues and bring on nosebleeds. High doses can lead to an irregular heartbeat, convulsions, stroke, hallucinations, and the sensation of worms or bugs crawling on the skin, known as formication. The use of Ritalin has also been associated with psychotic episodes.

Rohypnol

The first use of flunitrazepam (trade name Rohypnol) was in 1975 in European hospitals where deep sedation was needed. Its use spread to other countries. Although it is illegal in the United States, it has become a popular club culture drug. Reportedly, college and high school students use it to bring on intense drunkenness, to boost a heroin high, and to lessen the crash that may follow a heavy dose of cocaine or other stimulant.

Rohypnol is the drug most commonly referred to as the rape or date rape drug. It is a central nervous system depressant, a colorless, tasteless liquid that is easily mixed with alcohol and carbonated drinks. In alcohol it has a slightly bitter taste. Illegal in the United States, it is marketed by Hoffman-La Roche and is sold legally as a treatment for insomnia in Europe and Mexico. Since its illegal use as a date rape drug has surfaced, the manufacturer has attempted to make the drug easier to identify. The new forms of the drug turn blue in a light-colored drink and turn cloudy in a drink that is a dark liquid. However, not all forms on the illegal market have this blue dye.

The drug induces amnesia so that the victim of an assault may be unable to recall the events of the attack clearly. In this type of amnesia, the victim has difficulty remembering what happened while under

123

the influence of the drug. Such uncertainty may lead to a late report of a sexual assault by which time the drug may well have left the body.

Young people who use this drug reportedly have some misconceptions about it. They think that it is safe because it comes in bubble packs that are pre-sealed. Rohypnol is also said to be undetectable in the urine. Both ideas are wrong, although Rohypnol must be detected within seventy-two hours in order for doctors, rape counselors, and police to know definitively that someone has been given this drug.

NICD Classification of Rohypnol: *Depressant*
Scientific name: Flunitrazepam
Street names: Forget-me Pill, Lunch-Money Drug, Roach, Roofies, Rope, Rophies
How obtained: Rohypnol use is illegal in the United States and is obtained illicitly from drug dealers.
Medical uses: None in the United States. In the past, and in other countries, Rohypnol has been used to treat insomnia and as an hypnotic prior to the administration of anesthesia before surgery.
Illicit uses: Rohypnol has been used as a date rape drug. Illicit users sometimes take it to become intoxicated.
How taken: Rohypnol is usually consumed orally and mixed with liquids such as alcohol.
How Rohypnol works: Whether taken orally or ground into a powder and snorted, Rohypnol enters the bloodstream and activates the neuro-

transmitter, GABA. Rohypnol's activation of GABA slows down signals from the brain to the cardiovascular, respiratory, speech, motor, and cognitive centers, which slows down all related processes. The drug can cause decreased blood pressure, sleepiness, and even amnesia at higher doses.

Dependency potential: Some Rohypnol users develop a craving for the drug.

Interaction: Because Rophynol slows down many body functions, mixing it with other depressants such as alcohol, or anesthetics such as opiates and opioids, can result in coma and death.

Social dangers: Because Rohypnol affects higher brain centers involving judgment and slows down reaction time, speech, and motor centers, users may be unable to judge unsafe situations.

Legal dangers: The drug is classified under the Drug-Induced Rape Prevention and Punishment Act; its sale and/or possession can bring severe penalties.

Use and withdrawal symptoms: Symptoms include loss of motor control, slurred speech, confusion, and impairment of driving ability, among other skills. Higher doses can result in breathing difficulties.

GLOSSARY

ADHD—Attention deficit hyperactivity disorder, causing anxiety and inattentiveness.

aerosol—Any liquid substance in a metal container under pressure.

antibiotic—A chemical substance that inhibits or destroys bacteria.

antidepressant—A drug class of medications used to treat depression.

benzodiazepine—A depressant that slows down processes in the central nervous system.

blood-brain barrier—A cellular barrier that restricts passage of toxins, such as viruses and pathogens, into the brain.

cardiovascular—A body system affecting heart and blood vessels.

cirrhosis—A disease of the liver that increases scarred connective tissue.

club drugs—Illicit drugs that clubgoers use to intensify the music and dancing experience.

codeine—An opiate and the most widely used natural narcotic in medical treatment.

coma—A prolonged unconscious state brought on by disease, injury, or drug overdose.

date-rape drug—A colorless, tasteless substance that can be added to drinks to induce a state of near helplessness or inhibition in a victim.

dependency—A state of dependence on a drug or other substance to the extent that cessation may cause drug craving and withdrawal symptoms.

depressant—A drug that works on the central nervous system to relieve anxiety by slowing down some processes in the body.

euphoria—A state of enhanced well being as a result of drug usage.

GABA—Abbreviation of gamma aminobutyric acid, a major neurotransmitter in the brain that slows down signals between the brain and other parts of the body.

gateway drug—The first illicit substance a new drug user takes before moving on to other illicit drugs.

GHB—Abbreviation for gammahydroxybuty-rate, a depressant sometimes used as a date rape drug.

hallucinogen—A drug that alters a user's feelings and perceptions of reality.

heroin—The most rapidly acting of the opiates that induces a powerful state of euphoria and often leads to dependence.

hypnotic—A drug producing an artificially induced state of sleep.

inhalant—A chemical substance that gives off a vapor that can be breathed in.

marijuana—An illegal substance made of the hemp plant and smoked for its pleasurable effects.

metabolism—The physical chemical processes that give energy to the body.

methadone—A prescribed synthetic opiate used as a medication for heroin dependency.

morphine—A chief active ingredient in opium from which heroin is derived.

narcotic—Any class of a controlled substance that blunts the senses.

neurotransmitter—A chemical compound that sends signals between the brain neurons or nerve cells.

nicotine—A major ingredient in tobacco that affects the cardiovascular system and causes dependency in the user.

opiate—A narcotic made from the opium poppy and used as a sedative and pain reliever.

opioid—A synthetic narcotic that produces many of the same effects as natural opiates.

overdose—Excessive consumption of any chemical substance, often leading to damaging effects.

pharmacology—The science dealing with preparation and usage of drugs.

possession—Having illegal substances on one's person or in the home.

recreational drug—A drug used for its unintended purpose, such as getting high.

sedative—A medication for reducing anxiety or pain.

serotonin—A neurotransmitter responsible for mood swings and perceptional changes.

steroids—A large group of fat-soluble compounds including sex hormones.

stimulant—A drug used to increase alertness and energy.

tolerance—The duration of time before users experience symptoms.

withdrawal—The period after a drug is stopped, often with severe effects.

NOTES

Chapter 1

p. 17, par. 1, National Institute on Chemical Dependency (NICD) http://www.nicd.us/nicd drugclassifications.html

Chapter 2

Notes for sidebar: page 38
http://www.focusas.com/Alcohol.html

p. 39, par. 1, "Emergency Room Visits."
http://www.cdc.gov/alcohol/quickstats
/underage_drinking.htm
p. 44, par. 2, McCloskey, *When Winning Costs Too Much*, p. 25.

Chapter 3

Notes for sidebar: page 63
http://www.ncbi.nlm.nih.gov/sites/entrez?cmd=R
etrieve&db=PubMed&list_uids=11173173&dopt=
Abstract

p. 73, par. 1, "Huffing and Dusting,"
http://www.cbc.ca/health/story/1005/06/16
/huffing-dusting050616.html
p. 75, par. 1, "K-hole" www.urbandictionary-
com/define.php?term=k+hole, p. 1
p. 88, par. 5, *NIDA InfoFacts:Methamphetamine,*
National Institute on Drug Abuse, November 27, 2006,
http://www.nida/nih/gov/Infofacts/Methamphetamine.html,
pp. 1–2.

Chapter 4

1, "Effects of Opium, Morphine, and Heroin on
Addicts," *Consumers Union Report on Licit and Illicit
Drugs,* http://www.drugtext.org/library/reports/
cu/cu4.html, p. 12.
p. 98, par. 4, *John Rolfe* http://www.apva.org/history
/jrolfe.html, p. 1.
p. 99, par. 2, Ellis Paxson Oberholtzer, *A History of the
United States Since the Civil War,* p. iii.

Chapter 5
sidebar: p. 113
NIDA Community Drug Alert Bulletin – Inhalants
http://www.nida.nih.gov/InhalantsAlert/index.html,
p. 1, 3.

p. 111, par. 2, "Prescription drugs find place in teen culture," *USA Today*, November 24, 2006, p. 1.
p. 115, par. 1, *Substance Abuse and Mental Health Services Administration,*
http://oas.samhsa.gov/nsduh.htm, p. 4.

FURTHER INFORMATION

Books

Aaseng, Nathan. *Teens and Drunk Driving*. San Diego: Lucent, 2000.

Gerdes, Louise F. *Drunk Driving*. San Diego: Greenhaven, 2001.

Kittleson, Mark J., et al. *The Truth about Alcohol*. New York: Facts on File, 2005.

Landau, Elaine. *Date Violence*. New York: Franklin Watts, 2004.

Marshall, Sherry. *Young, Sober and Free*. Center City, MN: Hazelden, 2003.

Pellowski, Michael J. *Amphetamine Drug Dangers*. Berkeley Heights, NJ: Enslow, 2000.

Slayton, Elaine Doremus. *Empowering Teens*. Lake Forest, IL: Croya Press, 2000.

Williams, Mary E. *Marijuana*. San Diego: Thomson, 2003.

Web Sites
Child and teen abuse hotline.
http://www.childabuse.org/links.html
Date rape drugs.
http://www.scarleteen.com/crisis/drug_report.html
Drug abuse hotline.
http://www.addictioncareoptions.com/
Over-the-counter abuse.
http://www.teendrugabuse.us/
over_the_cunter_drug_abuse.html
Teen alcohol abuse. www.tarzanatc.org

Organizations for Help
Al-Anon Family Groups
1600 Corporate Landing Parkway
Virginia Beach, VA 23454
1 888 425 2666
http://www.al-anon.org

American Council for Drug Education (ACDE)
164 W. 74th St.
New York, NY 10023
800 488 DRUG (3784)
acde@phoenix.org
http://www.acde.org
Works with community members to help
    American teens avoid drug abuse

Children of Alcoholics Foundation
http://www.Coaf.org

Cocaine Helpline
800 cocaine (262 2463)

DanceSafe
1226 7th Ave #6
Oakland,CA 94606
dsusa@dancesafe.org
http://www.dancesafe.org

Hormone Foundation
8401 Connecticut Ave., Suite 900
Chevy Chase, MD 20815
1 800 Hormone
http://www.hormone.org

Leadership to Keep Children Alcohol Free
http://www.Alcoholfreechildren.org/gs/stats/

Mothers Against Drunk Driving (MADD)
511 E. John Carpenter Hwy, Suite 700
Irving, TX 75062
1 800 GET MADD
http://www.madd.org

New England Inhalant-Abuse-Prevention Coalition
58 Oak Ridge Road
Medford MA 02155
1 800 419 8398

Nicotine Anonymous
http://www.nicotine-anonymous. org

The QuitNet
http://www.quitnet.org

Partnership for a Drug-Free America
405 Lexington Ave, Suite 1601
New York, NY 10174
212 922 1560
http://www.drugfreeamerica.org

Students Against Destructive Decisions (SADD)
1-877-SADD-INC
http://www.saddonline.com

BIBLIOGRAPHY

Books

Edwards, Griffith, *Alcohol: The World's Favorite Drug.* New York: St. Martin's, 2002.

Hanson, David J., *Preventing Alcohol Abuse: Alcohol, Culture and Control.* Westport, CT: Praeger, 1995.

Henderson, Elizabeth Connell. *Understanding Addiction.* Jackson: University of Mississippi Press, 2000.

Griffith, H. W., *Companion Guide to Prescription and Non-Prescription Drugs.* New York: Penguin, 2006.

Ledda, Mary Ann, *Alcohol and Other Drugs.* Paramus, NJ: Globe Fearon, 1995.

Madison, Arnold, *Drugs and You.* New York: Messner, 1990.

McCloskey, John and Julian Bailes, M. D. *When Winning Costs Too Much: Steroids, Supplements and*

Scandal in Today's Sports. Lanham, MD: Taylor Trade, 2005.

Articles

The Association for the Preservation of Virginia Antiquities (APVA), "John Rolfe." http://www.apva.org/ history/jrolfe.html

Boal, Mark, "And It Was Perfectly Legal." *Rolling Stone.* 888. January 31, 2002.

Brecher, Edward and Editors. *Consumers Union Report on Licit and Illicit Drugs.* "Effects of Opium, Morphine and Heroin on Addicts." 1972.

Brown University. "Psilocybin." November 29, 2006. http://www.brown.edu/Student_Services/ Health_Services/Health_Education/ atod/ od _psilocybin.htm

Center for Disease Control Tobacco Information and Prevention Source (TIPS). "How to Quit." November 27, 2006. http://www.cdc.gov/tobac co/how2quit.htm

Center for Disease Control Tobacco Information and Prevention Source (TIPS). "You Can Quit Smoking Consumer Guide." December 1, 2006. http://www.cdc.gov/tobacco/quit/canquit.htm

Golub, Andrew Lang and Bruce D. Johnson,. "Alcohol Is Not the Gateway to Hard Drug Abuse." *Journal of Drug Issues.* 28 (4). Fall 1998.

Jackson, Marni. "Pass the Weed, Dad," *McLeans.* 118 (45). November 7, 2005. http://www.nida.nih.gov/MarjBroch/Marijteenst xt.html

McDermott's Guide to the Depressant Drugs. November 23, 2006, http://www.erowid.org/chemicals/opiates/opiates_mcdermotts_guide.shtml

Mosher, Clayton, et al. "Minority Adolescents and Substance Use Risk/Protective Factors: A Focus on Inhalant Use." *Adolescence San Diego.* 39 (155). September 18, 2006.

National Inhalant Prevention Coalition. "Damage Inhalants Can Do to the Body & Brain." (September 18, 2006). http://www.inhalants.org/damage.htm

National Institute on Drug Abuse. "Anabolic Steroid Abuse." NIH Publication (August, 2006). http://www.nida.nih.gov/ResearchReports/Steroids/AnabolicSteroids.html

National Institute on Drug Abuse. "Commonly Abused Drugs." (November 2006). http://www.nida.nih.gov/DrugPages/DrugsofAbuse.html

National Institute on Drug Abuse. "Hallucinogens and Dissociative Drugs," NIH Publication (March 2001). http://www.drugabuse.gov/ResearchReports/hallucinogens/hallucinogens.html

National Institute on Drug Abuse. "Heroin Abuse and Addiction." NIH Publication (May 2005). www.nida.nih.gov/ResearchReports/Heroin/Heroin.html

National Institute on Drug Abuse. "Inhalant Abuse." NIH Publication (September 2005). http://www.nida.nih.gov/InhalantsAlert/indiex.html

National Institute on Drug Abuse. "Marijuana: Facts for Teens." NIH Publication (September, 2006). http://www.nida.nih.gov/MarijBroch/ Marijteens.html
National Institute on Drug Abuse. "MDMA." NIH Publication. (March 2006.)
National Institute on Drug Abuse. "NIDA InfoFacts: Club Drugs." NIH Publication (September 2006). http://www.nida.nih.gov/infofacts/Clubdrugs.html
National Institute on Drug Abuse. "NIDA Infofacts: Marijuana." NIH Publication (November 2006). http://www.nida.nih.gov/Infofacts/marijuana.html
National Institute on Drug Abuse. "NIDA Infofacts: MDMA." NIH Publication (April, 2006). http://www.nida.nih.gov/Infofacts/ecstasy.html
National Institute on Drug Abuse. "NIDA InfoFacts: Methamphetamine." NIH Publication (November, 2006). http://www.nida/nih/gov/Infofacts/methamphetamine.html
National Institute on Drug Abuse. "NIDA Infofacts: PCP (Phencyclidine)." NIH Publication (November 2006). http://www.nida.nih.gov/Infofacts/PCP.html
National Institute on Drug Abuse. "NIDA Infofacts: Rohypnol and GHB." NIH Publication (November 2006). http://www.nida.nih.gov/Infofacts/RohypnolGHB.html
National Institute on Drug Abuse. "Prescription Drugs: Abuse and Addiction." NIH Publication (November 2006). http://nida.nih.gov/Research Reports/Prescription/prescription4.html
Partnership for Awareness. *Drug, Alcohol & Tobacco*

Awareness. "Mushrooms," November 29, 2006, http://www.partnershipforawareness.org /mushrooms.htm

Partnership for a Drug-Free America. "Ritalin Abuse/Ritalin Side Effects." November 24, 2006. http//www.drugfree.org/Portal/drug-guide/ Ritalin

Project GHB. "What is GHB?" November 24, 2006. http://www.projectghb.org/what_is_ghb.htm

Substance Abuse and Mental Health Services Administration, http://oas.samhsa.gov/nsduh.htm.

University of Virginia. "Timothy Leary." (February 1999) www.lib.virginia.edu/small/exhibits/sixties/leary.html

Urban Dictionary. "K-hole." http://www.urbandic-tionary.com/define.php?term=k+hole

USA Today. "Prescription Drugs Find Place in Teen Culture." November 24, 2006, http://www.usatoday.com /news/leath/2006-06-12- teens-pharm-drugs-x.htm

INDEX

Page numbers in **boldface** are illustrations, tables, and charts.

145

ABOUT THE AUTHOR

Corinne J. Naden is a former U.S. Navy journalist and children's book editor in New York City. The author of more than eighty books for young readers and adults, she lives in Tarrytown, New York.